The Mediterranean Diet Cookbook

101 Easy Recipe for Weight Loss

Table of Contents

CHAPTER 1 WHERE DID THE MEDITERRANEAN DIET COME FROM? WHY IS IT EFFECTIVE? 6

CHAPTER 2 THE RULES OF THE MEDITERRANEAN DIET 13
- PRODUCT COMPOSITION..15

CHAPTER 3 MEDITERRANEAN DIET MENU FOR A WEEK RECIPES 16
- MEDITERRANEAN DIET MENU FOR A wWEEK, THE RULES................................16
- MEDITERRANEAN DIET: RECIPES FOR WEIGHT LOSS 18

CHAPTER 4 MEDITERRANEAN DIET: BREAKFAST 21
- 1. GREEN FRITTATA 21
- 2. GENTLE SMOKED SALMON PATE 23
- 3. BREAKFAST BY GORDON RAMSAY 24
- 4. LUSH MEDITERRANEAN OMELETS 26
- 5. SPINACH PARADISE 27
- 6. MEDITERRANEAN WILD BERRY YOGURT 28
- 7. BLUEBERRY LIME SMOOTHIE 29
- 8. SUGAR-FREE DIET PANCAKES WITH CHOCOLATE SAUCE 30
- 9. BAKED HONEY PEARS 32
- 10. BANANA MINI PANCAKES WITH CINNAMON (NO EGGS).....................34
- 11. MILLET PORRIDGE WITH PUMPKIN CARAMEL 36
- 12. FRUIT OATMEAL 38
- 13. MEDITERRANEAN OATMEAL PIE WITH BANANAS AND BLUEBERRIES 40
- 14. RICE PUDDING WITH PUMPKIN 42
- 15. OATMEAL WITH BANANA AND COCOA 44
- 16. PORRIDGE WITH FRESH BERRIES 45
- 17. PUMPKIN AND ZUCCHINI PANCAKES 46
- 18. MUESLI BARS WITH CRANBERRIES AND COTTAGE CHEESE................48
- 19. COCONUT CASSEROLE 50
- 20. BAKED CHEESECAKES 52

CHAPTER 5 SALADS – MEDITERRANEAN KITCHEN...............................54
- 1. SALAD WITH ARUGULA AND SHRIMP 54
- 2. VEGETABLE SALAD WITH SHRIMP 56
- 3. COLD SALAD WITH GREEN BEANS..57

4. Diet seafood salad 58
5. Salad with tuna and fresh vegetables 59
6. Salad with octopus 61
7. Delicate sea lettuce 63
8. Green Salad with Smoked Trout, Capers and Horseradish Dressing ... 65
9. Kalmar with celery, olives, and shallots 67
10. Octopus carpaccio with a poke from avocado and tomatoes 69
11. Warm seafood salad from Jeremy Uryuti 71
12. Mediterranean Octopus Salad 73
13. Orange salad 76
14. Warm Salad of Baked Vegetables 77
15. Grilled Vegetables Salad 79
16. Tuna with Capers 80
17. Arugula with tuna in ginger-lime sauce 81
18. Salad with Squid and Pickled Onions 83
19. Mediterranean Shrimp Salad 85
20. Potato Salad without Mayonnaise 86

CHAPTER 6 - SOUPS - MEDITERRANEAN CUISINE- LOW-CALORIE FOOD 88

1. Soup-Puree of Lentils 88
2. Pumpkin Cream Soup with Shrimp 90
3. Cream Soup of Zucchini with Shrimp 92
4. Soup with Mussels 94
5. Easy Soup with Spinach 96
6. Chicken Soup with Dried Squid 100
7. Lentil Soup with Ginger, Tomatoes, and Cilantro 101
8. Seafood Soup with Crayfish tails 103
9. Cold Pea Soup with Shrimp 105
10. Mediterranean Broth 107
11. Salmon in green curry broth 109
12. Turmeric Lentil Soup 111
13. Cheese soup with shrimps and herbs 113

CHAPTER 7 - MEDITERRANEAN RECIPES MAIN DISHES 115

1. Sea Bass with Potatoes, Capers, and Tomatoes 115
2. Octopus with Artichoke, Tomato and Mint Sauce 117
3. Gilthead with Lemon 120
4. Mussels in the Mediterranean recipe 122

- 5. Sea Bass with Tomatoes and Italian Herbs 124
- 6. Carp, Baked with Walnuts, Pomegranate, and Spices 126
- 7. Shrimp with Ginger and Sherry 128
- 8. Grilled Marinated Halibut 130
- 9. Marinated in Lime Juice Grilled Shrimp in Wine Sauce 132
- 10. Octopus garnished with toasted lettuce 134
- 11. Sea bass stuffed with vegetables, mussels and saffron oil 136
- 12. Mediterranean Mussels with Thyme 138
- 13. Red mullet with Grappa 140
- 14. Lentils with greens 141
- 15. Salmon skewer with cherry tomatoes in a rosemary marinade 143
- 16. Stuffed Sardines On Skewers 144
- 17. Skewer of Norwegian Salmon 146
- 18. Lasagna with Turkey Meat and Bechamel Sauce 147
- 19. Sautéed Anchovies with Broccoli 150
- 20. Scallops In A Creamy Sauce with Mushrooms and Rice 152
- 21. Pork Stew with Celery, Carrots, Madeira Wine and Spices 154
- 22. Fillet of Seabass with Asparagus Wrapped in Bacon 156
- 23. Spaghetti Squash with Sun-Dried Tomatoes 158

CHAPTER 8 - MEDITERRANEAN RECIPES FOR SAUCES AND MARINADES 161

- 1. Lemon marinade with thyme and shallots for fish 161
- 2. Barbecue sauce for shrimp on the grill 163
- 3. Marinade with olive oil and herbs 165
- 4. The Marinade Made of White Wine with Oregano and Garlic 166
- 5. Garlic seasoning for grilled meat 167
- 6. Yogurt marinade with herbs and spices for Moroccan 168
- 7. Parsley oil 169

CHAPTER 9 SNACKS MEDITERRANEAN CUISINE 170

- 1. Spicy tomato dip to baked potatoes 170
- 2. Green beans with warm dressing and bacon 171
- 3. Rolls with lettuce 172
- 4. Baked tomatoes with Provencal herbs 173
- 5. Hummus with roasted peppers 174
- 6. Octopus Carpaccio 176
- 7. The Babaganoush with Roasted Peppers 178
- 8. Olives with Orange Zest, Cumin, and Caraway Seeds 180

9. CHEESE BASKETS WITH MUSSELS 181
  10. SCALLOPS UNDER THE PEAR PESTO 183
  11. ZUCCHINI IN GREEK 185

CHAPTER 10 DRINKS MEDITERRANEAN CUISINE 187
  1. SMOOTHIE PINEAPPLE RASPBERRY 187
  2. BEET-PINEAPPLE SMOOTHIE WITH FENNEL 189
  3. GRAPE SMOOTHIE WITH GREEN TEA 190
  4. BLACK CREAM SMOOTHIE 191
  5. BERRY CRANBERRY AND BLACKBERRY SMOOTHIE 192
  6. BLUEBERRY SHAKE WITH HONEY 193
  7. RASPBERRY COOLER WITH LEMON 194

CONCLUSION 195

Chapter 1 Where did The Mediterranean Diet Come From? Why is it Effective?

The Mediterranean diet is a collection of food principles and habits of the whole Mediterranean, which includes up to 16 countries. The basis of the Mediterranean diet are the cuisines of Spain, Italy, and Greece. Features of the cooking in this area formed the basis of a healthy diet, and a healthy diet as you know it.

On December 4, 2013, UNESCO decided to give the Mediterranean diet the status of an intangible cultural heritage from Italy, Portugal, Spain, Morocco, Greece, Cyprus, and Croatia.

The traditional cuisine for people from the Mediterranean countries is the use of a large number of seasonal vegetables and fruits, herbs, legumes, nuts, whole grain cereals, wholemeal bread, pasta made from durum wheat grains — the mandatory presence of olive oil in cooking - for frying, for dressing, greasing and pickling.

Regarding meat, such food as beef, veal, lamb, poultry are restraint, but regularity is traced. Pork is not famous, and it is rarely seen on the menu. Since this is a Mediterranean diet, a list is not complete without fish and seafood, being the primary source of polyunsaturated fatty acids Omega-3 and Omega-6.

As for dairy products, these are mainly sour-milk natural products like yogurt, low-fat yogurts, soft cheeses with low-fat content, for example, feta, mozzarella. Just milk or dairy dishes in the diet is a rarity. When the table is laid, then served with the red wine of excellent quality locally produced, in moderation.

Cakes, pastries, sweets are not fond of here. Preference is given to natural products like nuts, dried fruits, honey. People in this region lead an active lifestyle, are characterized by excellent optimism, are emotional, and have little susceptibility to disease. The secret is in many fundamental factors, but one of them is a healthy diet.

The term "Mediterranean diet" was introduced as a concept, back in the mid-twentieth century by American nutritionists, Case-Margaret and Anselmo. Based on studies of the lifestyle of the peoples of the Mediterranean, they built an organically food pyramid based on carbohydrates - 60%, followed by vegetable fats - 30%, proteins complete the structure, and makeup only 10%.

Product Benefits
If we consider the benefits that all products that make up the pyramid of food bring, then starting with the fruits and vegetables that make up its basis - we can say that all the valuable trace elements, vitamins, amino acids saturate the body to a sufficient extent.
It is recommended to use just seasonal vegetables, fruits, greens, which are grown and ripen naturally in the open ground.

Then only they retain valuable bioflavonoids, which are active antioxidants. And antioxidants are known to fight free radicals and slow down the aging process.

Minerals, such as selenium, manganese, zinc - are found in seafood, vegetables, and rice. They also inhibit oxidative processes in the body, which means that skin elasticity lasts longer. I especially want to note the benefits of olive oil, which is generously used in the Mediterranean diet. The oil should be used in the first extraction, unrefined, and then it fully preserves all the useful properties of olives, their aroma, and taste.

Monounsaturated fats found in olives have a very positive effect on the cardiovascular system, reduce the level of bad cholesterol LDL, and prevent the formation of blood clots in the vessels while making the walls of the ship secure. Olive oil can partially be replaced with any vegetable oil, and it is only essential that it be unrefined, cold-pressed. Low-fat meat of veal, beef, lamb supplies
the body with essential and necessary proteins, maintains the level of hemoglobin , and is involved in hematopoiesis.

The white meat of poultry, rabbit, is an easily digestible protein, a dietary product with low-fat content and a lack of carbohydrates. Lactic acid products are saturated with calcium available for assimilation, which strengthens bones, makes our hair healthy and strong teeth. Lactic acid also protects the intestines from infections, and organic acids contribute to the work of the digestive tract.

Red wine contains potassium, magnesium, iron, selenium, B, P, C vitamins - it strengthens the heart muscle, boosts immunity, and fights cancer cells. Therefore, its use in small quantities is beneficial. We will not ignore pasta and whole-grain cereals since they make up most of the nutrition of the inhabitants of the Mediterranean.

These are sources of complex carbohydrates that provide the primary energy to our body. If cereals are not processed, not polished, not refined, and pasta is made from durum wheat, then they are the wealthiest suppliers of fiber.

Chapter 2 The Rules of The Mediterranean Diet

To lose extra pounds and get rid of a high degree of risk of getting sick with the diseases accompanying overweight, the Mediterranean diet for weight loss is just what you need! Because it is already a way of life, and not only a temporary measure when you need to achieve the desired result quickly.

Consider the basic rules that should be followed, as well as products for the Mediterranean diet:
Every day you need to eat a lot of seasonal vegetables and fruits - this is the basis of all dishes, but potatoes need to be limited to 3 servings per week.

Dairy products - natural preparation with low-fat content. It is both simple and yogurts and soft cheeses. They are included in the daily diet. The diet should consist of seasonal fresh herbs, garlic, onions, spices - basil, rosemary, thyme, oregano.

Olive oil should take pride of place among all fats. Dress salads and dishes, preferably with first-pressed oil. Any other unrefined vegetable oil is also allowed.

Seafood, low-fat fresh fish (halibut, salmon, tuna, trout) - products included in the daily diet.

White meat - as mentioned above, eat in moderation, in small portions - 4 times a week, not more than 100 grams per serving. But red meat is allowed to eat no more than four times a month, that is, somewhere once a week.

Eggs - no more than once per day.

Pasta - only from durum wheat. Legumes, unprocessed rice, preferably brown, pearl barley, buckwheat - whole grains.

Drink enough water - it is the best non-alcoholic drink - 1.5 liters per day.

Red wine - served with dishes, no more than two glasses for women are drunk at a meal, and 3 glasses are allowed for men to drink.

Nuts, dried fruits, seeds should be eaten no more than one time per week. To exclude salt and flavorings from the diet as much as possible - it is better to use herbs and natural spices.

The ban applies to known non-useful foods - fatty meat, lard, flour sweets, confectionery, sweets, and ice cream.

Product Composition

Cereals - a source of fiber and carbohydrates. They are eaten in the morning.

Vegetables - consume fresh, seasonal, local products. The total mass can reach up to 1 kilogram per day. These are tomatoes, cucumbers, eggplant, zucchini and peppers, all kinds of salads: lettuce, arugula, iceberg, watercress, as well as olives, onions, and garlic.

Dairy products - natural yogurts, low-fat cottage cheese, and cheese combined with vegetables and fruits.

Fish and seafood - grilled, boiled, or steamed and served with lots of vegetables and herbs, pouring lemon.

Olive oil - used in salads, for frying and preservation. It contains polyphenols, antioxidants, and oleletanolamide, monounsaturated fatty acids.

Fruits and nuts - a traditional dessert.

Chapter 3 Mediterranean Diet Menu for a Week Recipes

Health, beauty, endurance — all of the inhabitants of the Mediterranean countries. What are the secret of their longevity and beautiful appearance? Perhaps influenced by the unique climate and healthy sea air. Not the last role plays and the specific Mediterranean diet. It is not surprising that this power system is becoming increasingly common around the world.

Mediterranean Diet Menu for a Week, the rules

The Mediterranean diet isn't to be confused with the cuisine of this region. The fact that among the traditional dishes a lot of calories and hearty, famous cheeses and sausages, pates and pasta, and sweet desserts with whipped cream and ice cream. Diet, by contrast, focused on more healthy and less calorie food. The foods that it includes, not only improve health and prevent the development of many diseases, but also help to lose weight and stay in great shape.

A typical list of products for compliance with the Mediterranean diet the following:

- fruits, vegetables, whole grains, low-fat dairy products daily;
- fish, seafood, lean meat — up to 5 times a week;
- eggs — up to 4 pieces in a week;
- lean red meat 1–2 times per week;
- wine — no more than two glasses a day.
- It is essential to remember the banned products, which include:
- fast food, processed foods;
- refined vegetable oils and cereals;
- sausage;
- products containing hydrogenated fats.

To follow the Mediterranean diet properly, consider these tips:
- Plant foods should prevail (whole grains, fruits, vegetables, nuts, legumes, cereals).
- As possible to limit the amount of red meat. Fish and poultry replace it.
- Instead of animal fats, use olive oil instead of frying cooked in the oven and steamed.
- Minimize the use of salt. Replace it with spices, spices, and herbs.
- Wine can be drunk at lunch and dinner, but not more than two glasses a day.

Here's what the weekly menu looks like following the recommendations of the Mediterranean diet.

Mediterranean Diet: Recipes for Weight Loss

You create your menu on your own. Then in the book, you will find 101 recipes for cooking dishes from Mediterranean cuisine for weight loss.

To adhere to this style of nutrition, you can use the sample menu for every day:

Monday:

- Breakfast - dietary pancakes without sugar with chocolate sauce;
- Snack - yogurt with banana;
- Lunch - grilled vegetables (tomatoes, zucchini, eggplant, bell peppers);
- Snack - fruit Mediterranean salad or vegetable salad
- Dinner - grilled fish with vegetables (tomatoes, broccoli, and bell peppers).

Tuesday:

- Breakfast - Spinach paradise;
- Snack - a salad with seafood;
- Lunch - baked salmon meat and vegetables (bell peppers, tomatoes, eggplant);
- Snack-. Mediterranean yogurt, «Wild berries. »
- Dinner - a low-calorie seafood dish, vegetables.

Wednesday:

- Breakfast - baked honey pears;
- Snack –crispbread with ham and hard cheese, cucumber;
- Lunch - cold pea soup with shrimp, vegetables;
- Snack - fruit smoothie or fruit yogurt;
- Dinner - vegetable salad seasoned with olive oil and a boiled seafood dish.

Thursday:

- Breakfast - yogurt with mashed berry, pistachios and pine nuts
- Snack - Greek yogurt and banana;
- Lunch - cheese soup with shrimp and herbs, vegetable juice
- Snack - mozzarella with rye bread;
- Dinner – a fish, baked with vegetables - dorado, pike perch or salmon, of your choice

Friday:

- Breakfast omelet with toast and fruit yogurt;
- Snack - Mediterranean smoothie with berries;
- Lunch - cold pea soup with shrimp tomato juice;
- Snack - nuts, banana;
- Dinner - grilled sea bass with potatoes.

Saturday:

- Breakfast - Mediterranean pie with oatmeal, bananas, and blueberries;
- Snack - a sandwich with ham and greens;
- Lunch - lentil soup puree;
- Snack - banana;
- Pasta dinner with shrimp and squid.

Sunday:

- Breakfast - lush Mediterranean omelet;
- Snack - grapefruit;
- Lunch - cream soup from zucchini with shrimp;
- Snack - fruit salad seasoned with yogurt;
- Dinner - lasagna with minced turkey and bechamel sauce

Chapter 4 Mediterranean Diet: Breakfast

1. Green Frittata

Serves: 2
Cooking Time: 20 minutes

ENERGY VALUE PER PORTION
- Caloricity 218 kcal
- Proteins 18.7 gram
- Fats 13.5 gram
- Carbohydrates 4.2 gram

INGREDIENTS
- Ground black pepper to taste
- Salt to taste
- A bunch Watercress
- A bunch Arugula
- A bunch Spinach
- A bunch Chives
- 4 Eggs

COOKING INSTRUCTIONS
1. Put chopped coarsely green onions in a pan and fry until soft. Add chopped greens and cook until it slightly fades.
2. Beat eggs with salt, pepper, and grated Parmesan. Pour into the pan. Cook over medium heat until baked from below.
3. Then put under the hot grill for several minutes until it rises. Immediately serve.

2. Gentle Smoked Salmon Pate

Serves: 4
Cooking Time: 30 minutes

ENERGY VALUE PER PORTION
- Caloricity 282 kcal
- Protein 9.2 gram
- Fats 26.3 gram
- Carbohydrates 3.2 gram

INGREDIENTS
- l2 tablespoons of Fennel
- 230g Mascarpone cheese
- 1 tablespoon Lemon juice
- 115g Smoked salmon
- Salt to taste
- Ground black pepper to taste

COOKING INSTRUCTIONS
1. In a blender, mix mascarpone cheese, chopped fennel, and lemon juice. Add half the finely chopped salmon and chop until smooth.
2. Transfer to a bowl and add the remaining finely chopped fish. Salt and pepper to taste

3. Breakfast by Gordon Ramsay

Serves 2
Cooking Time: 10 minutes

ENERGY VALUE PER PORTION
- Caloricity 272 kcal
- Proteins 11.1 grams
- Fats 20.1 grams
- Carbohydrates 10 grams

INGREDIENTS
- 2 Eggs
- 20g Butter
- 3 tbs Cottage cheese
- Salt to taste
- Black pepper hammers to taste
- 2 slices Rye bread

COOKING INSTRUCTIONS
1. Melt the butter in a small saucepan. Beat the eggs and pour them into the stewpan, mix with oil. Stir the eggs consistently over medium heat to prevent the mixture from solidifying from below. Add cottage cheese and mix thoroughly, allowing the cheese to dissolve.

2. When the mixture begins to thicken, remove the saucepan from the heat and continue stirring, the eggs will continue to set, thanks to the heated bottom. Add salt and pepper, and, if desired, seasonings to your taste or fresh herbs. If necessary, return the pan to the fire. Stir until the mass is thick enough, but still maintain a delicate, creamy consistency.
3. Simultaneously toast bread in a pot or a toaster. Serve toasts with eggs laid on top, add fried champignons, tomatoes or canned beans if desired

4. Lush Mediterranean Omelets

Serves: 2
Cooking Time: 30 minutes

ENERGY VALUE PER PORTION
- Caloricity 196 kcal
- Proteins 14.2 grams
- Fats 12.9 grams
- Carbohydrates 4.7 grams

INGREDIENTS
- 3 Eggs
- 170ml Milk
- Salami to taste
- Tomatoes to taste
- Salt to taste
- Chives to taste
- A mixture of ground peppers to taste
- Olive oil to taste

COOKING INSTRUCTIONS
1. Lubricate the bowl with olive oil, put tomato slices down (you can also lubricate with butter).
2. Then sausage and green onions.
3. Mix the eggs with milk, salt, and pepper, don't need to beat well.
4. Pour the eggs in the bowl and place in the oven. Bake at 200 degrees.

5. Spinach Paradise

Serves: 4
Cooking Time: 30 minutes

ENERGY VALUE PER PORTION
- Caloricity 115 kcal
- Proteins 5.8 g
- Fats 9.6 g
- Carbohydrates 0.5 g

INGREDIENTS
- 3 Eggs
- 25g Spinach
- 1 tbs Butter

COOKING INSTRUCTIONS
1. Break the eggs into a saucepan and beat slightly.
2. Mix finely chopped spinach with beaten eggs, salt and fry like a natural omelet.

6. Mediterranean Wild Berry Yogurt

Serves: 4
Cooking Time: 5 minutes

ENERGY VALUE PER PORTION
- Caloricity 159 kcal
- Proteins 6.7 gr
- Fat 8.9 g
- Carbohydrates 12.3 g

INGREDIENTS
- 100g Blueberries
- 100g Raspberries
- 450g Vanilla Yogurt
- 1tbs Ground pistachios
- 1tbs Roasted pine nuts

COOKING INSTRUCTIONS
1. In a blender, mix blueberries and raspberries and chop until mashed.
2. Arrange the yogurt in small bowls and gently pour the berry puree. Use a knife to make spiral-like movements in yogurt so that it partially mixes with mashed potatoes (do not mix thoroughly).
3. Sprinkle with pistachios and pine nuts on top.

7. Blueberry Lime Smoothie

Serves: 2
Cooking Time: 10 minutes

ENERGY VALUE PER PORTION
- Caloricity 186 kcal
- Protein 7.7 g
- Fats 5.6 g
- Carbohydrates 25.2 g

INGREDIENTS
- 2 cups Blueberries
- 3 cups Vanilla Yogurt
- 1½ tsp grated Lime zest
- 3 tbs of Lime juice
- 2 tbs Sugar

COOKING INSTRUCTIONS
1. Put the yogurt in several layers of cheesecloth and hang over a bowl for 30 minutes to dry slightly.
2. Meanwhile, in a saucepan, combine blueberries, lime zest, lime juice, and sugar. Put on medium heat and cook, stirring, for 2-3 minutes, until the berries begin to burst. Transfer to a bowl and refrigerate.
3. Before serving, mix yogurt with berries and serve.

8. Sugar-Free Diet Pancakes with Chocolate Sauce

Serves: 4
Cooking Time: 30 minutes

ENERGY VALUE PER PORTION
- Caloricity 162 kcal
- Protein 8 g
- Fat 6.1 g
- Carbohydrates 19.9 g

INGREDIENTS

- 1 cup Kefir
- 1 cup Oatmeal
- 2 Eggs

COOKING INSTRUCTIONS
1. Oat flakes should be chopped to the consistency of whole-grain flour.
2. Then mix all the ingredients. Make sure that there are no lumps left.
3. Put the dough in a pan with non-stick coating without oil and bake our pancakes on medium heat until they are completely covered with bubbles. After that, you can turn it over. Pancakes should turn out lush, golden.

TIP TO THE RECIPE
For baking such pancakes, I use an ordinary pancake pan and a tablespoon. Try not to do it very large; otherwise, it will be problematic to turn them over. But if you have such a kitchen "gadget" as a frying pan for pancakes, then you are lucky. Your pancakes will be perfectly smooth, and baking them will be much easier.

9. Baked Honey Pears

Serves: 8
Cooking Time: 40 minutes

ENERGY VALUE PER PORTION
- Caloricity 229 kcal
- Proteins 3.7 g
- Fat 10.7 g
- Carbohydrates 31.8 g

INGREDIENTS
- 1 cup Oatmeal
- ¼ cup Light brown sugar
- 70g Almonds
- ¼ tsp Ground cinnamon
- 50g Butter
- 3 tbsp Raisins
- 4 Pears
- Honey to taste

COOKING INSTRUCTIONS
1. Preheat the oven to 190 degrees.
2. In a bowl, mix oatmeal, brown sugar, almonds and cinnamon, mix. Add oil, stir until smooth. Add raisins.
3. Cut the pears in half (do not peel) and cut the core. Put the halves of the pears in a baking dish and grease the pears on top with melted butter.

4. Fill the middle of the pears with the oatmeal mixture prepared previously. Bake for 25 minutes until the pears are soft and the filling is slightly browned.
5. Pour honey and yogurt, serve warm for breakfast, or with ice cream for dessert.

10. Banana Mini Pancakes with Cinnamon (No Eggs)

Severs: 8
Cooking Time: 40 minutes

ENERGY VALUE PER PORTION
- Caloricity 57 kcal
- Protein 11 g
- Fats 22.6 g
- Carbohydrates 83 g

INGREDIENTS
- 1 Bananas
- 1 cup Milk
- ¾ cups Wheat flour
- ½ tsp ground cinnamon
- 2 tbsp Coconut oil

COOKING INSTRUCTIONS
1. Mix in a blender milk* and banana until smooth.
2. Add flour and cinnamon, mix (in the same blender, or a separate container).
3. Coconut oil to melt (but not overheat) and add to the dough. It can replace butter or vegetable, according to your taste.
4. Bake in a well-heated pan one tablespoon. Get little, tiny, adorable pancakes.
5. Ready pancakes go well with maple syrup and sweet tooth :)

TIP TO THE RECIPE
If you replace regular milk with almond, you get the same taste! The composition does not include sugar, as the perfect combination of ingredients — almond milk, banana, coconut oil, cinnamon — you won't need to. And the replacement products, you can add sugar to taste.

11. Millet Porridge with Pumpkin Caramel

Serves: 8
Cooking Time: 1 hour

ENERGY VALUE PER SERVING
- Caloric content 197 kcal
- Protein 6.4 g
- Fats 5 g
- Carbohydrates 33.7 g

INGREDIENTS
- 500g Pumpkin
- 250g Millet
- 500ml Milk
- 250ml Water
- 15g Butter
- 1 tsp Salt
- ½ tsp ground cinnamon
- 2 tbsp Sugar

COOKING INSTRUCTIONS
1. The pumpkin should be cleaned and cut into medium-sized cubes.
2. The butter should be melted in an active fire. You can use a large pot — one in which you will cook porridge.

3. When the butter has melted, add the pumpkin, a quarter spoon of salt, whole cinnamon, and 2 tablespoons sugar. Fry for 5-7 minutes until the distinct smell of pumpkin and caramel.
4. To roast the pumpkin, add all the prepared amount of milk, reduce the fire, and stew the pumpkin for 15-20 minutes under the lid.
5. Millet cereal washes thoroughly, first with cold and subsequently with hot water until the water after washing will not run clear. This is necessary to remove any chemical contamination and mealy coating with cereals, and the cooked rice is not bitter.
6. Add to the pumpkin millet cereal, remaining salt, and a Cup of water. Stir, cover, and cook for another 40-45 minutes. Occasionally lift the lid and stir the porridge. If all the liquid is absorbed before, and the millet will seem soft enough — add some more hot water.
7. In the finished oatmeal can add butter and sugar (or honey) to taste. Porridge cooked according to this recipe is delicious with walnuts and raisins.

12. Fruit Oatmeal

Serves: 1
Cooking Time: 1 hour

ENERGY VALUE PER PORTION
- Caloricity 32 kcal
- Protein 14 g
- Fat 9 g
- Carbohydrates 49.1 g

INGREDIENTS
- 6 tbsp Oatmeal
- 2 tbsp Oat bran
- Honey to taste
- ⅓ cups Natural yogurt
- Fruit to flavor
- ⅓ cups Milk

COOKING INSTRUCTIONS
1. Prepare a jar with a volume of 0.5 or 0.4 liters (You can use any container that is convenient for you with a lid)
2. Pour cereal, bran, yogurt, honey, and milk into a jar. Close the lid tightly and mix well, after adding freshly cut fruit
3. You can mix the ingredients in a separate bowl and then lay in a jar in layers, alternating oatmeal, and fruit.

4. Refrigerate for 3-4 hours, preferably all night. Enjoy a delicious breakfast

TIP TO THE RECIPE
Instead of milk, you can use just yogurt or kefir. If yogurt, then uses about 100 grams. If kefir, then in the same proportion as milk. For 100 g of the finished product without accounting for fruit, approximately 162 kcal

13. Mediterranean Oatmeal Pie with Bananas and Blueberries

Serves: 4
Cooking Time: 1 hour

ENERGY VALUE PER PORTION
- Caloricity 329 kcal
- Protein 9.1 g
- Fats 8.6 g
- Carbohydrates 5.6 g

INGREDIENTS
- 2 Bananas
- 1 cup Blueberries
- 3 tbsp Honey
- 20g Walnuts
- 1 cup Oatmeal
- 200ml Milk
- ⅓ tsp f Cinnamon
- 1 Egg
- 1 tsp Vanillin
- 1 tsp powdered Sugar

COOKING INSTRUCTIONS

1. Preheat the oven to 190 degrees. We take the dishes (I use a size of 25x15 cm), in which we will bake a cake. We cover the bottom and sides of the foil (if you have a ceramic dish, you need to grease it a little with oil - the foil is not necessary).
2. Cut the bananas into rings and put them in the prepared dishes.
3. There we add half the blueberries, 1/4 teaspoon of cinnamon, 1 tablespoon of honey, and cover with foil. Bake for 15 minutes until the bananas are soft.
4. Then, in a bowl, mix the oatmeal, half the walnuts, the baking powder for the dough and the remaining cinnamon, mix everything. In a separate bowl, beat the remaining honey, milk, eggs, and vanilla.
5. We get bananas with blueberries from the oven, sprinkle with an oatmeal mixture. Then evenly pour the mixture from milk. Sprinkle with the remaining blueberries and walnuts.
6. Bake the cake for about 30 minutes, or until a golden-brown crust forms on top. For decoration, sprinkle with powdered sugar. Serve warm.

14. Rice Pudding with Pumpkin

Serves: 8
Cooking Time: 1 hour & 40 minutes

ENERGY VALUE PER PORTION
- Caloricity 185 kcal
- Protein 8.1 g
- Fats 6.6 g
- Carbohydrates 25.2 g

INGREDIENT
- 1 kg Pumpkin
- ½ cups Rice
- 100ml Water
- 1 l Milk
- 2 Eggs
- 1 tsp Sugar

COOKING INSTRUCTIONS
1. Put the finely chopped or grated pumpkin into a saucepan, add water and cook until soft.
2. Add washed rice, milk to the pan, mix and cook for 30 minutes, then cool.
3. Then put everything in the patch, add beaten eggs and sugar. Mix everything.
4. Bake in the oven at 180-200 degrees until golden brown.

TIP TO THE RECIPE
The whole pudding is about 1480 kcal, and a portion of the piece is 185 kcal.

15. Oatmeal with banana and cocoa

Serves: 1
Cooking Time: 10 minutes

ENERGY VALUE PER PORTION
- Caloricity 270 kcal
- Proteins 10.8 g
- Fats 7.6 g
- Carbohydrates 42 g

INGREDIENTS
- ¼ cups of Oatmeal
- ⅓ cup of Milk
- ¼ cup of Natural yogurt
- 1 tbsp of Cocoa Powder
- 1 tsp of Honey
- ¼ of a Bananas

COOKING INSTRUCTIONS
1. Add oatmeal, milk, yogurt, cocoa powder, and honey to the jar.
2. Close the lid and shake well until all the ingredients are mixed.
3. Open, add slices of chopped ripe bananas and gently stir.
4. Close the top of the jar and put it in the refrigerator overnight (store up to 2 days). We eat oatmeal chilled.

16. Porridge with fresh berries

Serves: 1
Cooking Time: 20 minutes

ENERGY VALUE PER PORTION
- Caloricity 216 kcal
- Protein 2.8 g
- Fats 10.6 g
- Carbohydrates 27.5 g

INGREDIENTS
- 250ml of Water
- 1 tbsp of Buckwheat groats
- 1 tsp of Sugar
- 2 tbsp of Fresh berries
- 1 tsp of Butter

COOKING INSTRUCTIONS
1. Take 2 tablespoons of any fresh berries (raspberries, strawberries, currants, etc.), rinse, knead a crush, squeeze the juice through cheesecloth. Boil the squeeze in 200–250 ml of water and strain.
2. Put 1 tablespoon of cereal (buckwheat or semolina) into the broth, cook until cooked, add 1 teaspoon of sugar and butter, let it boil again.
3. Remove the porridge from the stove and pour the squeezed juice into it.

17. Pumpkin and zucchini pancakes

Serves: 2
Cooking Time: 20 minutes

ENERGY VALUE PER SERVING
- Calories 189 kcal
- Proteins 10.2 g
- Fat 4.1 g
- Carbohydrates 34.2 g

INGREDIENTS
- 1 Zucchini
- 400g Pumpkin
- 2 tbsp of Wheat Flour
- 1 Egg
- 1 tsp of Starch
- Salt to taste
- Vegetable oil to taste
- Sour cream to taste

COOKING INSTRUCTIONS
1. Grate the pumpkin and zucchini on a coarse grater. Add salt, leave on for 3-5 minutes so that the vegetables gave the juice. Squeeze and drain excess liquid, so you don't have to put extra flour.
2. Add the flour, starch, egg, and mix well.
3. Preheat the pan on medium heat, grease with oil.

4. Tablespoon spread each pancake into the pan.
5. When one side appears Golden brown, flip and press with a spoon. You can do this maneuver several times to pancakes thoroughly.

18. Muesli bars with cranberries and cottage cheese

Serves: 12
Cooking Time: 40 minutes

ENERGY VALUE PER PORTION
- Caloricity 93 kcal
- Protein 4,5 g
- Fat 2.3 g
- Carbohydrates 148 g

INGREDIENTS
- 200g of Oatmeal
- 200g of Soft cottage cheese
- 100g of Cranberries
- 2 tbsp of Honey
- Salt pinch
- 1 tsp of Cinnamon
- ¼ tsp Lemon zest
- 2 Eggs

COOKING INSTRUCTIONS
1. Knead oatmeal (less fine grinding and minimal conditioning), soft cottage cheese, add egg, honey, salt, cinnamon, zest.
2. Gently, with a silicone spatula, introduce berries into the mixture (cranberries can be replaced with any other, whether it be currants, raspberries, blueberries, etc.)

3. Take a flat baking sheet, put parchment paper on it , or grease it with oil. Put the resulting mass and distribute it in the form of a rectangle or square (so that it is convenient to cut into portions).
4. Bake at 200 degrees for 15-20 minutes. As soon as the mass becomes sufficiently elastic - grease with the yolk.
5. Having taken out freshly baked muesli, immediately (while they are soft) cut into portions with a knife.

You can serve or let them cool (about 2-3 hours or even leave overnight)

19. Coconut Casserole

Serves: 8
Cooking Time: 1 hour

ENERGY VALUE PER SERVING
- Calories 191 kcal
- Proteins 14.1 g
- Fats 8 g
- Carbohydrates 17.3 g

INGREDIENTS
- 500g of Soft low-fat cottage cheese
- 180g of Sour cream
- 3 tbsp Sugar
- 50g of Coconut
- 2 Egg
- 1 Bananas
- 50g of Fresh berries
- 2 tbsp Wheat flour

COOKING INSTRUCTIONS
1. Mix the sugar and eggs.
2. Add cheese and sour cream, mix until smooth.
3. Add the flour (preferably sifted) and mix well to avoid lumps.
4. Then enter the coconut.
5. Pour the mixture into the baking pan.
6. Bake for 35 minutes at 180 degrees.

7. Serve casserole warm or chilled. You can decorate with banana slices or berries.

TIP TO THE RECIPE

Fresh berries and banana are used to decorate the finished dish.

20. Baked cheesecakes

Serves: 9
Cooking: 1 hour

ENERGY VALUE PER PORTION
- Caloricity 142 kcal
- Protein 7.6 g
- Fats 4.6 g
- Carbohydrates 19.4 g

INGREDIENTS
- 300g of Soft cottage cheese
- 2 Bananas
- 1 Egg
- 1 cup of Wheat bran
- 65g of Roasted Peanuts
- 3 tbsp Ground cinnamon

COOKING INSTRUCTIONS
1. Pound bananas in mashed potatoes.
2. Pour the cottage cheese over the banana puree and mix well.
3. Beat the egg and mix thoroughly with the mixture.
4. Add cinnamon, mix.
5. Cover the baking sheet with parchment paper and put the cheesecakes on it.

6. Bake in the oven at 180 degrees for about 40-60 minutes (depending on the stove) until a good golden brown.

TIP TO THE RECIPE

Wheat bran can be replaced with oat bran. If the consistency is dehydrated (but it should not turn out that way), then you can add quite a bit of kefir.

Chapter 5 Salads – Mediterranean Kitchen

1. Salad with Arugula and Shrimp

Serves: 2
Cooking Time: 20 minutes

ENERGY VALUE PER SERVING
- Calories 472 kcal
- Protein 17.2 g
- Fats 41.2 g
- Carbohydrates 5.9 g

INGREDIENTS
- 100g of Shrimp 100 g
- 2 Garlic cloves
- 70ml of Olive oil 70 ml
- 20ml of Red wine
- 20ml of Balsamic vinegar
- 30ml Dry white wine
- 65g of Spicy arugula " White cottage "
- 40g of Parmesan cheese
- Salt to taste
- Ground black pepper to taste

COOKING INSTRUCTIONS
1. A mixture of butter and olive oil sauté shrimp for 1-2 minutes, add the chopped garlic, as soon as the aroma, pour in the wine and evaporate for 30 seconds, then remove from heat.
2. Mix red wine and balsamic vinegar with olive oil, pepper, and salt with a beater. Mix the arugula with the sauce.
3. On a plate , put the salad, her shrimp, pour wine sauce from the pan, decorate with slices of Parmesan, salt, and pepper.

2. Vegetable salad with shrimp

Serves: 4
Cooking Time: 15 minutes

ENERGY VALUE PER PORTION
- Caloricity 185 kcal
- Protein 24.4 g
- Fats 7.9 g
- Carbohydrates 4.4 g

INGREDIENTS
- 500g of Boiled , peeled shrimp
- 3 Tomatoes
- 20ml of Olive oil
- 2 Cucumbers
- Salt to taste

COOKING INSTRUCTIONS

1. Tomatoes and cucumbers cut into cubes.
2. All together with the shrimp mix. Add salt to taste and add olive oil.

3. Cold salad with green beans

Serves: 2
Cooking Time: 25 minutes

ENERGY VALUE PER SERVING
- Calories 81 kcal
- Protein 4.1 g
- Fat 3.2 g
- Carbohydrates 9.0 g

INGREDIENTS
- 500g of Peeled, boiled shrimp
- 3 Tomatoes
- 20ml of Olive oil
- 2 Cucumbers
- Salt to taste

COOKING INSTRUCTIONS

1. Beans boil in salted water, cold.
2. The cherry tomatoes cut into halves, season with salt, drizzle with olive oil, spread on a baking sheet, and put in 4-5 minutes in the preheated oven. Cool.
3. Olives cut into halves.
4. Prepare the filling — mix the olive oil, salt, black pepper, herbes de Provence, and lemon juice.
5. Mix all ingredients, season.

4. Diet seafood salad

Serves: 2
Cooking Time: 10 minutes

ENERGY VALUE PER PORTION
- Caloricity 105 kcal
- Protein 16.5 g
- Fat 2.2 g
- Carbohydrates 4.2 g

INGREDIENTS
- 50g Crab sticks
- 50g Canned mussels
- 50g Small peeled, boiled shrimp
- 50g Gherkins
- 50g Canned squid
- 20g Natural yogurt
- 10g Fennel
- 2ml Balsamic vinegar
- 3g Salt with herbs

COOKING INSTRUCTIONS
1. Finely chop all the ingredients.
2. Salt with yogurt, vinegar, and mix in a bowl. Season the salad, layout , and garnish with dill.

5. Salad with tuna and fresh vegetables

Serves: 4
Cooking Time: 15 minutes

ENERGY VALUE PER PORTION
- Caloricity 142 kcal
- Protein 11.4 g
- Fat 9 g
- Carbohydrates 4.7 g

INGREDIENTS
- 200g Canned Tuna
- 1 English cucumber
- 2 Pink tomatoes
- 2 Yellow tomatoes
- 10g Chives
- 10g Red basil
- 30ml Extra virgin olive oil
- 20g Olives
- 5g Ground black pepper
- 5g Sea salt
- 5g Sesame

COOKING INSTRUCTIONS
1. Vegetables a good wash.
2. Cucumber, tomatoes cut into cubes, chop the herbs, olives — circles. Put all ingredients in a bowl. Mix with olive oil, salt, and pepper. Put on a plate slide.

3. Tuna recommend taking in a glass jar, so you can see the fish itself. Fish chopped coarsely and spread on top of the salad. Sprinkle with sesame seeds to decorate and give texture to the mixture.

6. Salad with octopus

Serves: 2
Cooking Time: 30 minutes

ENERGY VALUE PER PORTION
- Caloricity 229 kcal
- Proteins 28.2 gram
- Fats 10.2 gram
- Carbohydrates 8.3 gram

INGREDIENTS
- 300g Octopus
- ½ Red onions
- 250g Tomatoes
- 1 tbsp Olive oil
- 1 tbsp Vinegar

COOKING INSTRUCTIONS
1. First, finely chop the onion, and we scald it with boiling water. This simple procedure will remove the bow from the anger. Pour the boiling water and pour the onion with a spoon of vinegar.
2. Boil water for octopus (add lemon, salt, pepper, rosemary, and everything you love to seafood).
3. As soon as the water boils - put in a pan of octopus and cook until tender. I had a small, boiled three minutes.

4. Cut the tomatoes shorter. Add to them the greens (I added Basil, parsley, and coriander).
5. Get the octopus and chop them.
6. Mix all ingredients and fill lettuce with salt, pepper, olive oil, and a splash of balsamic vinegar.

7. Delicate sea lettuce

Serves: 5
Cooking Time: 25 minutes

ENERGY VALUE PER PORTION
- Caloricity 121 kcal
- Proteins 14.7 g
- Fats 4.5 g
- Carbohydrates 6.8 g

INGREDIENTS
- 450g Frozen mussels
- 300g Green beans (frozen)
- 300g Frozen broccoli cabbage
- 200g Cucumbers
- 30g French mustard
- 10ml Olive oil
- 20ml Soy sauce
- 2g Mixture of ground pepper
- 20g Green onion feathers

COOKING INSTRUCTIONS
1. Put frozen mussels in a preheated pan and simmer for 5 minutes without oil, then drain the juice and water into the sink, transfer to a salad bowl.

2. Defrost green beans and broccoli under running water or in advance on the top shelf of the refrigerator (the same can be done with mussels).
3. Large inflorescences of broccoli cut into small pieces, cut the cucumbers into strips. Transfer beans, cabbage, and cucumbers to molds.
4. Chop finely chopped green onion, add to salad.
5. Add mustard, olive oil, and soy sauce to taste. The combination of these three ingredients gives a unique special taste.
6. You can also add salt and pepper to taste, mix.

8. Green Salad with Smoked Trout, Capers and Horseradish Dressing

Serves: 4
Cooking Time: 10 minutes

ENERGY VALUE PER PORTION
- Caloricity 75 kcal
- Protein 12 g
- Fat 1.1 g
- Carbohydrates 7.2 g

INGREDIENTS
- 1 Lettuce
- 400g Watercress
- 1 cup mixture of lettuce leaves
- 120g Smoked trout
- 100g Avocado
- 1 tbsp Capers
- 1 Red onions

COOKING INSTRUCTIONS
1. In a large bowl, mix chopped lettuce, watercress , and a mixture of salad leaves with aromatic dressing with horseradish . Avocado should be diced
2. Arrange on 4 plates. Top with sliced fish, sprinkle with green onions and capers.

9. Kalmar with celery, olives, and shallots

Serves: 6
Cooking Time: 25 minutes

ENERGY VALUE PER PORTION
- Caloricity 289 kcal
- Protein 41.6 g
- Fat 11.2 g
- Carbohydrates 6.3 g

INGREDIENTS
- ⅓ cups Olives
- 1 Celery stalk
- 3 pieces shallots
- 1 tsp Lemon zest
- 1 tbsp Lemon juice
- ¼ cup Olive oil
- 3L Water
- 500g Squid
- 1 tbsp Salt

COOKING INSTRUCTIONS
1. Rinse squid carcasses in cold running water and cut into thin rings. Tentacles cut in half along.

2. Boil water by adding 1 tablespoon of salt. For 40 seconds, throw the squid in boiling water, and then immediately place it in an ice container. When the squids cool, remove them from the ice and throw them in a colander to drain all the water from them.
3. Meanwhile, cut celery stalks, green olives, and shallots into thin rings. Mix with freshly grated lemon peel, olive oil, and lemon juice.
4. When the squid stops dripping water, they can be combined with the rest of the ingredients.
5. Serve the salad chilled or at room temperature.

10. Octopus carpaccio with a poke from avocado and tomatoes

Serves: 1
Cooking Time: 20 minutes

ENERGY VALUE PER PORTION
- Caloricity 279 kcal
- Proteins 25.3 g
- Fats 16.5 g
- Carbohydrate 7.5 g

INGREDIENTS
- 120g Octopus
- 20g Arugula
- 5g shallots
- 5g Parmesan cheese
- 2g Frize salad
- 8ml Olive oil
- 10ml Balsamic vinegar
- 2g Sea salt
- 1g Ground black pepper
- 30g Tomatoes
- 30g Avocado
- 20g Citronet sauce
- 1 Shallot
- Balsamic cream to taste

COOKING INSTRUCTIONS
1. Rinse the octopus carcass thoroughly, boil, peel, and cut into slices. Cut the tomatoes and avocado coarsely and season with balsamic cream.
2. Put an octopus on a pillow of arugula, sliced with parmesan, shallots, and celery.
3. Season with citron sauce (to prepare, mix one part of olive oil and half a lemon juice, salt, and pepper).
4. Serve with a poke from tomatoes and avocados.

11. Warm seafood salad from Jeremy Uryuti

Serves: 1
Cooking Time: 30 minutes

ENERGY VALUE PER PORTION
- Caloricity 326 kcal
- Protein 24.5 g
- Fat 6.8 g
- Carbohydrates 24.6 g

INGREDIENTS
- 30g Scallops
- 45g Octopus
- 40g Frozen shrimp
- 20g Green peas
- 30g Broccoli cabbage
- 20g Kenyan beans
- 30g Mini asparagus
- 5g Butter
- 1ml Truffle oil
- 20ml Truffle sauce

COOKING INSTRUCTIONS
1. Vegetables (broccoli, peas, Kenyan beans) cook separately. Dip asparagus in boiling water for 15 seconds. To keep the plants bright green, put them on the ice for 1 min after cooking.
2. Prawn, octopus, and scallop with salt, pepper, and fry in butter.
3. Serving: put vegetables on a plate, put seafood on top in the center, pour with truffle oil. Serve truffle sauce separately in a gravy boat.

12. Mediterranean Octopus Salad

Serves: 4
Cooking Time: 2 hours

ENERGY VALUE PER PORTION
- Caloricity 358 kcal
- Proteins 39.1 g
- Fats 13.9 g
- Carbohydrates 20.2 g

INGREDIENTS
- 2 pieces Octopus
- 4 Potato
- 20g Chives
- 3 tbsp Extra virgin olive oil
- 1-piece Lemon
- 3 tbsp Salt
- Ground black pepper to taste
- 1 clove Garlic
- 20g Parsley

COOKING INSTRUCTIONS

1. If the octopus is fresh, it must be cleaned: cut into 3 parts - tentacles, "face" and head. The face should be thrown out, the arms should be removed from the substantial part connecting them, the head should be turned inside out, and all the insides removed. Rinse. Frozen octopus - you need to slowly defrost it in the refrigerator, most likely it has already been cleaned.
2. Bring to a boil 4 liters of water with 3 tablespoons of salt. Each part of the octopus is immersed in water for 10 seconds, removed, let the water boil again and repeat the procedure 2 more times. Thus, the tentacles of the octopus will curl beautifully, and the meat will be more tender. Then cook all the parts over low heat for an hour. Drain the water in which the octopus was boiling, and let it cool in the water at room temperature.
3. Now the colorful and slightly slippery skin of the octopus can be easily cleaned with fingers. In Italy and Portugal, they leave her, but here you need to rely on your taste and preference for texture. Cut the octopuses with diagonal pieces of 2-3 cm. Try for salt - if salt is not enough, then add salt.

4. Mix the octopuses with oil, lemon juice, parsley, onions, garlic. Mix well and leave at room temperature for about an hour (in such a marinade, the octopus can live in the refrigerator for 2 days). 5. Meanwhile, cook the potatoes and cut them into 1.5–2 cm cubes.
5. Serve until the vegetables have cooled entirely by mixing with the octopus in the marinade.

13. Orange salad

Serves: 1
Cooking Time: 20 minutes

ENERGY VALUE PER PORTION
- Caloricity 198 kcal
- Proteins 27.4 g
- Fat 2.4 g
- Carbohydrates 17.6 g

INGREDIENTS
- 250g Frozen shrimp 250
- 150g Crab sticks
- 1 Tomatoes
- 1 Sweet pepper
- ½ Red onion
- Parsley leaves
- Salt to taste
- Ground black pepper to taste

COOKING INSTRUCTIONS
1. Defrost the shrimp by boiling them in salted hot water for 5 minutes.
2. Grate crab meat on a coarse grater, chop the bell pepper into strips, tomatoes - in small cubes, add a little onion, salt, pepper.
3. Add parsley leaves. Mix.

TIP TO THE RECIPE
You can add parsley or dill and decompose portions on lettuce.

14. Warm Salad of Baked Vegetables

Serves: 4
Cooking Time: 2 hours

ENERGY VALUE PER PORTION
- Caloricity 199 kcal
- Proteins 7.5 g
- Fat 7.2 g
- Carbohydrates 27.1 g

INGREDIENTS
- 3 Eggplant
- 4 Yellow bell pepper
- 4 Red bell pepper
- 2 Zucchini
- 2 Fennel
- 2 Red onion
- 5 branches Dill
- 5 branches Parsley
- 5 branches Cilantro
- 4 cloves Garlic
- 2 tbsp Olive oil
- 1 tbsp Provencal herbs
- 1 tsp Lemon juice
- ½ tsp Sea salt

COOKING INSTRUCTIONS
1. Cut eggplant lengthwise into eights, put on a baking sheet, lightly sprinkle with olive oil, sprinkle with salt.
2. Bake in a preheated oven (250 ° C) for 20 minutes until golden brown. Transfer to a salad bowl.
3. Reduce oven temperature to 220 ° C.
4. Peel and finely chop the garlic.
5. Remove seeds from sweet pepper, cut each into eights as well, spread on a baking sheet, drizzle with olive oil, sprinkle with sea salt, half Provence herbs, and garlic, and bake in the oven for 10-15 minutes until tender.
6. Put pepper in a colander to stack excess juice.
7. Zucchini thinly cut and put on a baking sheet.
8. Cut fennel and red onion into eight slices, add to the zucchini, sprinkle with olive oil, salt, and sprinkle with the remaining Provence herbs.
9. Bake in the oven for 8-10 minutes until the fennel is ready, then cool to room temperature. Finely chop the greens.
10. Put the baked vegetables in a salad bowl to the eggplant, mix, sprinkle with lemon juice or apple cider vinegar, sprinkle with herbs.

15. Grilled Vegetables Salad

Serves: 4
Cooking Time: 1 hour

ENERGY VALUE PER PORTION
- Caloricity 108 kcal
- Protein 7.1 g
- Fat 1.7 g
- Carbohydrates 17.5 g

INGREDIENTS
- 2 Eggplant
- 2 Zucchini
- 2 Sweet pepper
- 2 Cucumbers
- 150g Natural yogurt
- 3 cloves Garlic
- 2 tsp f Lemon juice
- Salt pinch
- Ground black pepper to taste

COOKING INSTRUCTIONS
1. Eggplant and zucchini cut into circles.
2. Grease with olive oil, bake on the grill.
3. Cucumber cut into slices, pepper into cubes.
4. Slices of eggplant and zucchini in half.
5. Mix yogurt with finely chopped garlic and lemon juice. 6. Mix all the vegetables in a bowl, salt, and pepper, pour the dressing.

16. Tuna with Capers

Serves: 2
Cooking Time: 15 minutes

ENERGY VALUE PER PORTION
- Caloricity 88 kcal
- Protein 14.6 g
- Fat 1.1 g
- Carbohydrates 5 g

INGREDIENTS
- ½ bunch of Green salad
- 120g of Canned tuna in its juice
- 10 Cherry tomatoes
- 20g Pickled capers
- Salt to taste
- Balsamic sauce to taste
- 1 Cucumbers

COOKING INSTRUCTIONS
1. Tomatoes and cucumber cut into 4 parts, sectors. Break the salad, split the tuna into small pieces, add capers, salt, mix.
2. Top with balsamic sauce.

17. Arugula with tuna in ginger-lime sauce

Serves: 2
Cooking Time: 15 minutes

ENERGY VALUE PER PORTION
- Caloricity 419 kcal
- Proteins 33.9 g
- Fats 26.7 g
- Carbohydrates 11 g

INGREDIENTS
- 240g Tuna fillet
- 80g Arugula
- 100g Avocado
- 4 Quail egg
- 80g Cherry tomatoes
- 1 Lime
- 10g Ginger root
- 15g Caper
- 30g Olives
- 20g Pickled pearl onions
- 15g Granular mustard
- 4g Sugar
- 20ml Olive oil
- Salt to taste

COOKING INSTRUCTIONS

1. With 0.5 lime, remove the zest and squeeze the juice, mix with butter from dried tomatoes (40 grams).
2. Add mustard, sugar, ginger sliced into thin strips, salt.
3. Thoroughly mix with a whisk until salt and sugar are completely dissolved; put the sauce in the refrigerator.
4. Boil quail eggs in copiously salted water for 6 minutes; fresh in running cold water; peel.
5. Peel the avocado from the skin and cut into a giant cube; cut the flesh of the olives from the stone.
6. Fry the tuna in a hot frying pan in olive oil on each side for 2 minutes, salt, cut into 8 parts.
7. Put the arugula in the center of the plate, place the tuna pieces next to it, cut in half cherry and quail eggs, capers, pearl onions, avocado cubes, black olives; pour arugula and tuna sauce and serve.

18. Salad with Squid and Pickled Onions

Serves: 4
Cooking Time: 1 hour

ENERGY VALUE PER PORTION
- Caloricity 403 kcal
- Protein 28.4 g
- Fat 22.9 g
- Carbohydrates 21.2 g

INGREDIENTS
- 200g Squid
- 2 Onion
- 1 Yellow bell pepper
- 1 Tomatoes
- 2 Cucumbers
- 12 pitted olives
- 125g Natural nonfat yogurt
- 4 tbsp Olive oil
- 1 tsp Mustard
- ½ a Lemon
- Ground black pepper to taste
- 4 tbsp Vinegar
- ½ a beam of Dill
- Salt to taste
- 1 tbsp Sugar

COOKING INSTRUCTIONS
1. Remove the zest from half a lemon and grate.
2. Dill and chop 1 tablespoon of chopped dill.
3. Peel the onion, cut into thin half-rings, put in a bowl ,and sprinkle with dill.
4. Mix a glass of cold boiled water, 4 tbsp. 9% vinegar, 1 tbsp. Salt and 1 tablespoon sugar, pour the resulting mixture of onions. Close the bowl tightly and refrigerate for 30 minutes.
5. Wash squid by removing the thin outer film and chitin plates. Dip in boiling salted water for 2 minutes. Lean back into a colander and let cool.
6. Wash the tomato and cucumbers. Remove the core from sweet pepper. Cut vegetables into small cubes, put them in a bowl.
7. Squid cut into strips.
8. Drain the marinade from the onion. Onions, along with squid and olives, add to vegetables.
9. Beef yogurt, olive oil, and mustard for the dressing. Add lemon zest, salt, and pepper. Pour the salad and mix.

TIP TO THE RECIPE
The recipe can use squid canned in its juice.

19. Mediterranean Shrimp Salad

Serves: 4
Cooking Time: 30 minutes

ENERGY VALUE PER PORTION
- Caloricity 104 kcal
- Protein 13.1 g
- Fat 4 g
- Carbohydrates 4.6 g

INGREDIENTS
- 1 Tomatoes
- 250g of Shrimp
- 2 Cucumbers
- Ground black pepper to taste
- 50g of Light Cream
- 1 tbsp of Cream cheese

COOKING INSTRUCTIONS
1. Boil shrimps pour over cold water and clean. Cut each shrimp in half.
2. To prepare the cheese sauce, mix processed cheese (preferably Viola) and 20% cream until a homogeneous consistency is obtained.
3. Cut the cucumbers. Put cucumbers, shrimps on a typical dish, add sauce, black pepper, and mix. Cut a tomato and decorate it with a salad.

20. Potato Salad without Mayonnaise

Serves: 4
Cooking Time: 1 hour

ENERGY VALUE PER SERVING
- Calories 189 kcal
- Protein 3.7 g
- Fat 6.3 g
- Carbohydrates of 30.9 g

INGREDIENTS
- 6 Potatoes-
- 4 stalks Spring Onion
- 60g Gherkins
- 1 tbsp Grainy mustard
- 1 cup vinegar
- 1 tbsp Olive oil
- 1 tsp Sugar
- Salt teaspoon
- 1 tsp f Black pepper

COKING INSTRUCTIONS
1. Peel the potatoes and slice. Transfer to a pan and pour water so that it covers it completely, then bring it to a boil. Reduce the heat and simmer until tender about 20 minutes. Drain the water and rinse the potatoes under cold water flow to cool.

2. In a large bowl, whisk mustard, vinegar, olive oil, salt, pepper, and salt.
3. Add the cooled potatoes, green onions, and gherkins.
4. Stir and leave in the fridge until the time of serving.

Chapter 6 - Soups - Mediterranean Cuisine- Low-Calorie Food

1. Soup-Puree of Lentils

Serves: 6
Cooking Time: 30 minutes

ENERGY VALUE PER PORTION
- Caloricity 201 kcal
- Proteins 12.2 g
- Fats 0.7 g
- Carbohydrates 33.8 g

INGREDIENTS
- 300g Red lentils
- 1 Onion
- 1 Tomatoes
- 2 Carrot
- •2 cloves Garlic
- 3 slices White bread
- 10g Ginger root

COOKING INSTRUCTIONS
1. Boil lentils.
2. Coarsely chop the onions and tomatoes.
3. Grate the carrots coarsely. Ginger - finely.
4. Finely chop the garlic.
5. Fry all vegetables in a pan.
6. Add to the pan to the lentils.
7. Simmer for 10-15 minutes.
8. Grind everything with a blender.
9. Cut the bread into small cubes and fry without oil in a pan over low heat for 10 minutes, continually stirring.

2. Pumpkin Cream Soup with Shrimp

Serves: 6
Cooking Time: 1 hour

ENERGY VALUE PER SERVING
- Calories 312 kcal
- Protein 19.5 g
- Fat 15.2 g
- Carbohydrates 34.6 g

INGREDIENTS
- Pumpkin pieces
- 200ml Light Cream
- Salt to taste
- 10 Tiger prawns
- 3 Cloves Garlic
- Ground black pepper to taste
- 50g Butter
- Herbs to taste

COOKING INSTRUCTIONS
1. Pumpkin cut into pieces of 2x2 cm Cook until tender, add the greens and garlic. Once the pumpkin is ready, grind it, puree (I use a hand blender — faster and more efficiently), add the cream, and put on a small fire for a few minutes.

2. At this point, the butter with the garlic fry shrimp a few minutes until the prawns turn pink and are covered with a small blush.
3. In a bowl put the shrimp, pour the soup on top.

3. Cream Soup of Zucchini with Shrimp

Serves: 1
Cooking Time: 30 minutes

ENERGY VALUE PER SERVING
- Calories 232 kcal
- Proteins 23.8 g
- Fat 5.5 g
- Carbohydrates 25.7 g

INGREDIENTS
- 1 Zucchini-
- 2 cups Broccoli
- Bow rapacity head
- 1 cup Green beans
- 1 Carrots
- Salt to taste
- 200g Shrimp
- 100g Cream cheese
- Spices to taste

COOKING INSTRUCTIONS
1. Washed and cut into large pieces boil vegetables (you can vary the number and interchangeable these vegetables in the recipe for the squash, cauliflower and, etc.) in water. Once it boils, add salt and spices to the soup to taste.

2. In parallel with the vegetables in a separate pan, cook the prawns with salt and lemon juice (also to taste).
3. Once the shrimp are ready, they need to be cooled, throwing in a colander.
4. From ready-made vegetables is also necessary to drain the water and move them in a blender, then add cream cheese (you can Fetaki, but in this case, add less salt), cut into cubes, and mix everything thoroughly until a homogeneous, creamy mass.
5. Pour into bowls and decorate with peeled shrimp.

4. Soup with Mussels

Serves: 6
Cooking Time: 50 minutes

ENERGY VALUE PER SERVING
- Calories value of 335 kcal
- Proteins 26.9 g
- The fats 18.3 g
- Carbohydrates 13.7 g

INGREDIENTS
- 1.5kg Mussels
- 100ml Dry white wine
- Thyme
- 1 Bay leaf
- 3 tbsp Olive oil
- 150g Onions
- 1 clove garlic
- 3 tbsp Potato starch
- 500ml f Milk
- 2 Egg yolk
- Parsley
- Salt to taste
- Ground black pepper to taste

COOKING INSTRUCTIONS
1. Open mussels with a knife blade and remove algae and other nonsense. Then rinse them under cold water. Remove any molds with damaged shells and those that do not slam when they touch. Put the mussels in a saucepan, pour in the wine and add the thyme, Bay leaf and a pinch of salt. Cover with a lid and cook over high heat, occasionally shaking the pan, for 6 minutes, until all shells open.
2. Remove mussels with a slotted spoon and remove all that remain closed.
3. Pour the broth from the mussels through a fine sieve into a clean bowl and set aside. Remove the molds from the shells; place them on a plate, and cover, so they don't dry.
4. Heat the olive oil in a pan, add finely chopped onion and crushed with the flat side of the blade the garlic cloves. Fry it on a slow fire, occasionally stirring, 5 minutes until they are soft. Add 1.5 liters of water and the broth from the mussels and cook for 10 minutes. Starch, mix with six tablespoons of water, and pour it into the soup. Cook for another 5 minutes, then add hot milk. Add salt and pepper to taste.
5. In a tureen, put the egg yolks and slowly pour the soup, so the egg yolks do not brew into lumps. Add mussels, if very large, cut them into two parts. Sprinkle soup with chopped parsley. Serve immediately.

5. Easy Soup with Spinach

Serves: 3
Cooking Time: 35 minutes

ENERGY VALUE PER SERVING
- Calories 252 kcal
- Protein 7.1 g
- Fat 21.5 g
- Carbohydrates 8.8 g

INGREDIENTS
- 200g Spinach
- 1 Onions
- 11/2 cloves of Garlic clove
- 2½ cups Broth
- ½ Light Cream
- 1 rounded tsp of Black pepper
- 1 tbsp Olive oil
- Salt to taste

COOKING INSTRUCTIONS
1. Using a knife for cutting raw vegetables, peel the skin of onions and garlic cloves. Then iterate through and remove from a bundle of spinach is damaged and eaten by intersecting leaves, throws the rest of the greens in a colander ,and rinse under cold running water along with the vegetables.

2. After the dried onion and garlic, paper kitchen towels, and leave the spinach in the colander for 5 – 7 minutes to drain excess liquid.
3. Then alternately stacked vegetables with herbs on a cutting board and cut the onion into strips or half rings with a thickness up to 5 mm, finely chop the garlic, spinach leaves, leave whole or cut in 2-3 pieces. Spread the chopped vegetables on individual plates. Also, put on the kitchen table the olive oil, salt, cream, ground black pepper, broth, or vegetable broth.
4. Now, turn the stove to medium level and put it on a nonstick pan with 1 tablespoon of olive oil. When the oil heats up, drop in chopped onions. Simmer the vegetables until light Golden brown and transparent, occasionally stirring wooden kitchen spatula. After 3-4 minutes, add to the pan the chopped garlic and simmer them together for another 1 minute while stirring intensively, as much time is necessary to ensure that pieces of garlic dissolve his spicy scent.
5. After you enter in the pan the spinach leaves, season them with ground black pepper, salt and simmer with vegetables until soft. This process will take no more than 3-4 minutes.
6. When the leaves of greens shrink, pour into a saucepan 2.5 cups of broth or vegetable broth. Then bring the liquid to a boil, turn off the stove and allow the mixture to cool to room temperature.

7. When the soup is cooled, pour the contents of the pan into a clean and dry blender jar. Grind until a homogeneous liquid mass is obtained at the highest speed, it will take no more than 2 minutes.
8. Then again, pour the mixture in the same nonstick pan and put it on the stove included in the average.
9. After 1-2 minutes, pour into a saucepan half a glass of liquid cream, mix 2 tablespoons of liquid until smooth, taste for flavor, and, if necessary, add more salt and black pepper. Heat the soup to 90 degrees; thus, don't allow it to boil, so the cream does not curdle.
10. When on the surface of the soup will appear the first bubbles, turn off the stove, cover the pot with a lid and allow the first hot dish to infuse for 4-5 minutes. Then, using a spoon, pour the soup plates and served to the dining table.
11. Soup-puree of spinach served hot for dinner. It is possible to add croutons, homemade croutons of any bread you can also sprinkle each serving of soup shredded Parmesan cheese or fresh finely chopped dill, parsley, green onions. Very often, this soup seasoned fried bacon or braised meat. Enjoy!

TIP TO THE RECIPE
The set of spices listed in this recipe can be supplemented with any seasonings that are suitable for the preparation of the first hot or vegetable dishes, such as savory, sage, rosemary, paprika, white pepper, black pepper and these are only a few of all the possible options. Instead of heavy cream, you can use low-fat cream. Optional onions and garlic to stew with carrots and mushrooms, these ingredients complement the taste and flavor of the finished soup.

6. Chicken Soup with Dried Squid

Serves: 4
Cooking Time: 1 hour

ENERGY VALUE PER SERVING
- Caloric 295 kcal
- Proteins to 38.8 g
- Fats 3 g
- Carbohydrates, 27.8 g

INGREDIENTS
- 2 Chicken breasts
- 150g Spaghetti
- 5 tbsp Dried squid
- Chopped parsley to taste
- Potato chips to taste
- Coarse salt to taste

COOKING INSTRUCTIONS
1. Cut the chicken breast into bite-size pieces.
2. In the broth to boil pasta or broken thin spaghetti.
3. Add the chopped chicken and dried squid.
4. Season with salt to taste.
5. Serve with chopped parsley and potato chips.
6. In 3 liters of water to boil 2 chicken Breast.

7. Lentil Soup with Ginger, Tomatoes, and Cilantro

Serve: 4
Cooking Time: 50 minutes

ENERGY VALUE PER SERVING
- Calorific value 338 kcal
- Proteins 13.3 g
- Fats 6.4 g
- Carbohydrates of 57.9 g

INGREDIENTS
- 30g Onions
- 5g Garlic
- 280g Lentils
- 30g Fresh ginger
- 5g Chili pepper
- 5g Basil
- 20ml Olive oil
- 2g Salt
- 1.2L Water
- 300g Tomatoes
- 5g Cilantro
- 300g White bread
- 2g Black pepper powder

COOKING INSTRUCTIONS

1. Finely chop tomatoes, onion, garlic, ginger, and chili and fry in olive oil. It the end of cooking, add to the lentils, and when the beans become Golden brown, add water, and then cook. Cooking time was determined as the lentils, and it should soften. In the end, add the diced tomatoes and decorate the soup with coriander leaves.
2. You can now start making brackets — hot bread is the perfect complement to the soup, but preparing it in a matter of seconds! Prepared white bread place in the oven and bake until crisp. The rest of the tomatoes cut by cubes, add the shredded Basil, garlic, and salt, focusing on the taste, pour olive oil and mix thoroughly.
3. It remains to put the received weight on a loaf of hot bread and serve with soup!

8. Seafood Soup with Crayfish tails

Serves: 8
Cooking Time: 40 minutes

ENERGY VALUE PER SERVING
- Calories 359 kcal
- Protein 34.4 g
- Fats 20.2 g
- Carbohydrate 10.7 g

INGREDIENTS
- 1 tbsp Vegetable oil
- 4 cloves Garlic
- 1 Onion
- 1 Green peppers-
- 2 cups Fish stock
- 4 cups Coconut milk
- 1½ tbsp Chopped Basil leaves
- 1 tbsp Freshly chopped oregano leaves
- 5g Fresh sage
- 2 tsp Sugar
- 500 g river cancer
- 1½ tsp Ground cumin is
- 200g Squid
- 300g Mussels in shells
- 200g Shrimp
- Salt to taste
- Ground black pepper to taste
- 1-piece Lime

COOKING INSTRUCTIONS
1. On medium heat, fry chopped onion, garlic, and bell pepper until soft.
2. Add the coconut milk, broth, finely chopped Basil, oregano, sage, cumin, sugar to boil.
3. Reduce heat, add peeled and diced crawfish tails (leave some for garnish), sliced squid, and cook under the lid until soft, about 5-7 minutes.
4. Add the tails of shrimp and washed mussel shells. Cover and cook until shells of mussels open, about 7 minutes. Season with salt and pepper, serve with slices of lime, garnish with the boiled crayfish.

9. Cold Pea Soup with Shrimp

Serves: 4
Cooking Time: 40 minutes

ENERGY VALUE PER SERVING
- Caloric value 255 kcal
- Proteins 22.6 g
- Fats: 5 g
- Carbohydrates 35.1 g

INGREDIENTS
- 30g Cilantro leaves (coriander)
- 1 can Canned green peas
- 1 clove Shallot Onion
- 5 cloves Garlic
- 1 Green sweet pepper,
- 2 Chili pepper-
- Mint
- 1 tsp Coriander seeds
- 100g Sour cream
- 2 tbsp Lemon juice
- Ground black pepper to taste
- Salt to taste
- 300g Shrimp

COOKING INSTRUCTIONS
1. Clean and boil shrimp. Slice the vegetables. Chop the herbs and leave some for decoration.
2. Fry the garlic, onion, coriander seeds, and chili in a small amount of vegetable oil.
3. Add bell pepper and about a Cup of water, salt, and pepper. Simmer until tender.
4. Move contents of skillet to the blender; add peas, greens, sour cream, and lemon juice. Grind to a puree.
5. Soup cooling. Garnish with shrimp, herbs, and serve.

10. Mediterranean Broth

Serves: 6
Cooking Time: 40 minutes

ENERGY VALUE PER SERVING
- Caloric value 865 kcal
- Proteins 68.5 g
- Fats: 29.9 g
- Carbohydrates 52.6 g

INGREDIENTS
- 500ml White dry wine
- 1L Chicken stock
- 1 Garni bouquet
- 1 Carrot
- 1 Leek
- 1 Onion
- 4 Black allspice
- 1 Lemon
- 1kg Fish
- 3 Crayfish
- 300g Shrimp
- Saffron pinch
- 5 Champignons
- 10g Parsley
- Salt to taste
- Ground black pepper to taste

COOKING INSTRUCTIONS
1. Chicken broth diluted with one liter of water and a glass of dry wine, throw in the pan with the food, the Bouquet Garni, finely chopped carrots, onions, mushrooms, leeks, and pepper. Put on fire, bring to boil, reduce the heat slightly, and gurgling able to hold on the stove for about twenty minut
2. Then immerse in a pot with the broth fish and cook for ten minutes. Next, we have to add crawfish, shrimp, a pinch of saffron, squeeze lemon juice, season with salt and pepper and cook for another two to three minutes after the soup comes to a boil again.
3. Now you need to remove the pan from the heat, with a slotted spoon to remove from the soup, fish, and shrimp on a separate plate. Strain the broth through a fine sieve and serve in fishplates or bowls, sprinkle with finely-chopped parsley.

TIP TO THE RECIPE
One of the types of the famous Marseilles soup is called Bouillabaisse. It is in a lot of different seafood, which is cooked and eaten separately from the broth. As a sauce for fish, you can mix the olive oil, lemon juice, crushed garlic, salt, chopped parsley, dill, and black pepper. The sauce you can pour over the fish or add it to the broth.

11. Salmon in green curry broth

Serves: 4
Cooking Time: 52 minutes

ENERGY VALUE PER PORTION
- Caloricity 299 kcal
- Protein 31.2 g
- Fats 13.8 g
- Carbohydrates 11.3 g

INGREDIENTS
- 1 tsp Coriander seeds
- 1 tbsp Vegetable oil
- Turmeric pinch
- Pinch caraway seeds
- 2 Chili pepper
- 2 pieces Shallot onions
- 2 cloves Garlic
- 2 tbsp Grated ginger
- 30g Green onion feathers
- 1 piece Lime zest
- 3 tbsp Lime juice
- 1 tsp Coarse salt
- 3 cups Chicken broth
- Ground black pepper to taste
- 500g Salmon fillet
- 210g Spinach
- 2 tbsp Chopped cilantro (coriander)
- 1 tbsp Ground mint leaves
- 1 tbsp Shredded basil leaves

COOKING INSTRUCTIONS

1. On medium heat fry for a minute, the coriander and cumin in vegetable oil. To make the fire stronger and add turmeric, crushed chilies, coarsely chopped shallots, chopped garlic and ginger, chopped green onions, lime zest, and lime juice. Sauté for 3-4 minutes.
2. In a saucepan, bring to boil broth, salt, and pepper. Add the food, the entire mixture from the pan, and cook for another 3-5 minutes.
3. Strain the mixture through a fine sieve into a clean saucepan, pushing all the rest and once again bring the broth to a boil over low heat.
4. Add salmon, diced, and cook it to desired doneness, 5 to 7 minutes.
5. Add the chopped spinach and chopped herbs. Serve immediately

12. Turmeric Lentil Soup

Serves: 4
Cooking Time: 45 minutes

ENERGY VALUE PER SERVING
- Calories 324 kcal
- Proteins 19.1 g
- Fat 3.9 g
- Carbohydrates 49.8 g

INGREDIENTS
- 3 cloves Garlic
- 300g Red lentils
- 50g Ginger
- 2 tsp Turmeric
- Salt to taste
- 100 ml cream
- 1 Tomatoes
- 2 Carrots
- 1 Onions-

COOKING INSTRUCTIONS
1. Soak the lentils overnight. For soups and chowder is better to take Persian red lentils or yellow - they are better than other soft. Soak the lentils need here is why: all legumes contain phytic acid, which impedes getting into our body heaps of useful nutrients like calcium, complicating metabolism. Soaking removes this problem.

2. Boil the lentils for one hour.
3. While it cooks: chop the onion, and remove the skin from the tomato and chop (it is enough to hold it under the boiling water for 10 minutes), beautiful grate carrots, and ginger.
4. Fry the vegetables, adding them to the skillet with a difference of 5 minutes in this order: onion, carrot, ginger, tomato.
5. Then add seasonings. This can be done in two ways. First longer: at the bottom of the clean pan, put the butter, pressed garlic, after two minutes, the turmeric. Fried in butter seasoning better reveal their flavors. So, they don't burn, pour in the buttercream. And then the lentils, which pre-drain to the water. Second method: if too lazy to dirty another pan, you can drain the lentils with water, add the cream and add all the seasoning directly into the beans.
6. Cook the lentils with the spices for another 20 minutes.
7. Put in the lentil's vegetables. Boil another 10 minutes.
8. Grind the entire blender.
9. Served with pumpkin seeds and toasted bread.

13. Cheese soup with shrimps and herbs

Serves: 4
Cooking Time: 45 minutes

ENERGY VALUE PER SERVING
- Calories 339 kcal
- Proteins 34.2 g
- Fat 12.6 g
- Carbohydrates 51 g

INGREDIENTS
- 15 pieces of Shrimp
- 400g Cream cheese
- 1 Carrots
- 1 clove Shallot Onions
- 4 Potatoes
- 1 Garlic
- Salt to taste
- Spices to taste

COOKING INSTRUCTIONS
1. Chop the garlic, onion, and carrot and fry in a pan until desired softness.
2. In two liters of boiling water to melt the grated cheese, adding it a tablespoon and stirring constantly.
3. Salt, add spices to taste.
4. In cheese broth and throw sliced potatoes.

5. When the potato is cooked, remove from heat and add to the soup roasted mixture of carrots, onions, and garlic and chopped greens.
6. Fresh shrimp pre-cleaned in a separate bowl, pour a small amount of hot soup ready.
7. Pink shrimp to add to soup before serving.

TIP TO THE RECIPE

Keep the shrimp in a separate bowl. If you throw them in a pot of soup or overexpose in hot water (more than 3 minutes), they will become rubbery.

Chapter 7 - Mediterranean Recipes Main Dishes

1. Sea Bass with Potatoes, Capers, and Tomatoes

Serves: 6
Cooking Time: 1 hour & 10 minutes

ENERGY VALUE PER SERVING
- Calorie 692 kcal
- Proteins 66,3 g
- Fats 35,2 g
- Carbohydrates 22.7 g

INGREDIENTS
- 2kg Sea bass
- 600g Potatoes
- 400g Cherry tomatoes
- 30g Capers
- 200ml Dry white wine
- 1 Lemon-
- 20g Parsley
- 4 cloves Garlic
- 150ml Olive oil

COOKING INSTRUCTIONS

1. Cut the potatoes into slices 5 mm thick and boil in salted water. Drain in a colander, then dry with paper towels and mix with 50 ml of olive oil.
2. Pour on a baking sheet and put in an oven preheated to 180 degrees for thirty minutes. Add the chopped in half tomatoes, washed the salt from the capers, put the gutted fish, salted her and pepper. Drizzle the contents of the pan 50 ml of olive oil, wine, and send it in the oven for another half hour.
3. When serving, remove the fish fillet from the bones, put on a plate of potatoes with capers and tomatoes, sprinkle the fish with lemon juice and parsley and garlic butter (parsley, garlic and 50 ml of butter are pounded in a blender for two minutes and strain through a fine sieve).

2. Octopus with Artichoke, Tomato and Mint Sauce

Serves: 1
Cooking Time: 40 minutes

ENERGY VALUE PER PORTION
- Caloricity 896 kcal
- Protein 62.7 g
- Fat 51.1 g
- Carbohydrates 37.9 g

INGREDIENTS
- 1 Artichokes
- 1 Tentacle Octopus
- 3 Tomatoes
- 1 Carrot
- 1 clove Garlic
- 50ml Olive oil
- 70ml White dry wine l
- Thyme to taste
- Fresh mint
- 30ml Lemon juice
- Salt to taste
- Ground black pepper to taste
- 3 Cherry Tomatoes

COOKING INSTRUCTIONS

1. Cut the top of the artichoke so that it can be securely put on the Board. Cut off the tough outer leaves, then remove and discard the fuzzy core and some internal purple leaves, cut off the stalk. Pour all the slices with lemon juice and place in a bowl with cold water.
2. Clean the carrots and cut them into small cubes. Blanch the tomatoes in boiling water, then peel, and two of them are precisely the same cut. At the last turn to chop the artichoke. Octopus put in a saucepan, pour water and put to boil on medium heat for twenty to twenty-five minutes.
3. In a small skillet, heat olive oil, throw the diced artichoke, add lemon juice (it can be squeezed directly by the hands of half a lemon), stir and fry for a couple of minutes
4. Add to the artichoke carrots and tomatoes, salt, black pepper, thyme, and chopped garlic, stir and cook all together for another two minutes. Then pour the wine over low heat to let the liquid boil away. Well, if the vegetables will retain their shape and density.
5. In the bowl of a blender, put the remaining peeled tomatoes, add mint leaves (leaving a few pieces for decoration) , and blend until smooth. Boiled octopus drain in a colander and dry.

6. Sauté the octopus in a small frying pan in olive oil on all sides for three to four minutes or until light golden brown (fry the octopus for a long time is not necessary, otherwise it will become tough).
7. On a serving dish, put two tablespoons of the vegetable mixture on top of each portion gently lay the fried octopus tentacle.
8. Pour each serving with a small amount of sauce of tomato and mint, then sprinkle with chopped mint leaves. And serve immediately.

TIP TO THE RECIPE

Artichokes — the noble relatives of Thistle with edible unopened inflorescence after they are processed instantly darken the sections. To preserve the color, they need to be watered lemon juice.

3. Gilthead with Lemon

Serves: 2
Cooking Time: 30 minutes

ENERGY VALUE PER SERVING
- Calorie 726 kcal
- Proteins of 73.4 g
- Fats 47,2 g
- Carbohydrates 5.5 g

INGREDIENTS
- 2 Dorado
- 1 Lemon
- 2 Bay leaves
- 70ml Olive oil
- 1 tbsp Paprika
- Salt to taste

COOKING INSTRUCTIONS
1. The fish is cleaned, gut, wash thoroughly inside and out. Dry with a paper towel and rub a small amount of salt. Lemon cut in half; one half to be postponed, the second cut into thin circles. Put in the internal cavity of each fish 2-3 Cup of lemon and 2 leaves of Laurel. Preheat the oven to 190 C.

2. The pan cover with a sheet of parchment. Mix olive oil with paprika. Put the fish on a baking sheet and generously pour this mixture. Place in oven and bake for 10 min. Ready to pour the juice squeezed from the remaining half lemon, and immediately serve.

4. Mussels in the Mediterranean recipe

Serves: 2
Cooking Time: 20 minutes

ENERGY VALUE PER SERVING
- Calorie 877 kcal
- Protein 51 g
- Fats 63.3 g
- Carbohydrate 10.7 g

INGREDIENTS
- 500g Mussels
- 1 cup Dry white wine
- 2 tbsp Olive oil
- Bow
- 2 cloves Garlic
- 200g Cheese
- 1 tbsp Chopped parsley
- 200ml Cream

COOKING INSTRUCTIONS
1. A little sauté in olive oil chopped onion and garlic. Then put this mixture was pre-thawed mussels, hold them on the fire and add the wine.
2. When the alcohol is half evaporated, add the cheese, parsley, and black pepper.
3. Wait till the cheese melts in wine, add eye cream, bring to the boil and remove from heat.

TIP TO THE RECIPE
It can be used as mussels in shells and purified. If you put in the dish, the Parmesan, turn the molds in Parmesan sauce. If you use Gorgonzola or Dor-blue - creamy seafood. The recipe can be submitted white wine and toast, rubbed with garlic , and fried in olive oil.

5. Sea Bass with Tomatoes and Italian Herbs

Serves: 1
Cooking Time: 30 minutes

ENERGY VALUE PER SERVING
- Calorie532 kcal
- Protein 29g
- Fats 45.1g
- Carbohydrate 2.8g

INGREDIENTS
- 150g Sea bass
- 40ml Olive oil
- 5g Anchovies
- 1g Oregano
- 30g Zucchini
- 30g Cherry tomatoes
- 2g Rosemary
- Salt to taste
- 1g f Freshly ground white pepper

COOKING INSTRUCTIONS
1. Fillet of seabass marinated with Italian herbs, black and white ground pepper for 10 minutes. Zucchini and cherry tomatoes fried in olive oil.
2. In a baking dish, put the cooked vegetables, put the sea bass fillets and bake in the oven for 10 minutes at 180 ° C. When serving the finished dish to put in the center of the plate, garnish with anchovies, lemon and herbs.

6. Carp, Baked with Walnuts, Pomegranate, and Spices

Serves: 6
Cooking Time: 1 hour

ENERGY VALUE PER SERVING
- Caloric value 308 kcal
- Protein 19.8 g
- Fats 22.3 g
- Carbohydrates 9.4 g

INGREDIENTS
- 1 Carp
- 1 cup Crushed walnut
- 1 cup Pomegranate seeds
- 1 Onions
- Salt to taste
- Ground red pepper to taste
- 1 tbsp Olive oil

COOKING INSTRUCTIONS
1. Fish is cleaned, gut, wash in cold running water, RUB with salt, and leave for 30 minutes.
2. Onions and walnuts grind in a food processor.
3. Add the onion mixture with nuts spices, pomegranate seeds, and stir.

4. Lubricate the carcass of a carp with oil, place on a foil sheet, stuff cooked mixture, wrap in foil and send to 15 minutes in an oven preheated to 190 degrees. Then unwrap the foil and leave in oven for another 5-7 minutes until golden brown.
5. Serve with lemon and greens.

7. Shrimp with Ginger and Sherry

Serves: 1
Cooking Time: 15 minutes

ENERGY VALUE PER SERVING
- Calorific value 561 kcal
- Proteins 28,9 g
- Fats 43,1 g
- Carbohydrates 4.5 g

INGREDIENTS
- 150g of Peeled shrimp
- 2 tbsp of Butter
- 1.5 tsp of grated ginger
- 2 tbsp of Sherry
- 2 tbsp of Cilantro
- Salt to taste
- Ground black pepper to taste

COOKING INSTRUCTIONS
1. Rinse shrimp in cold running water, dry and sprinkle with salt.
2. In a frying pan of medium size with a heavy bottom to heat on medium heat the butter. Then throw in the grated ginger and sauté 30 seconds.
3. After the ginger to send to the pan, the shrimp and fry 2 minutes.
3. Pour into the pan with shrimp and ginger sherry and continue to cook for another 2 minutes.

4. Add to pan with roughly chopped cilantro, season with salt and pepper, and mix well.
5. Serve with a baguette. As a side dish - green beans.

8. Grilled Marinated Halibut

Serves: 8
Cooking Time: 25 minutes

ENERGY VALUE PER SERVING
- Calories 194 kcal
- Proteins 19.9 g
- Fats 10.5 g
- Carbohydrates 5.5 g

INGREDIENTS
- 1 Onion
- 800g Halibut
- 2 tbsp Wheat flour
- 2 tbsp Ghee
- 1 bunch Parsley
- 1 Lemon
- Salt to taste
- Ground black pepper to taste
- 10ml Vinegar

COOKING INSTRUCTIONS
1. Turbot meat is divided into 8 portioned pieces with the skin but without bones. Each salt and pepper, sprinkle finely chopped onions and drizzle with vinegar. Refrigerate for two hours.
2. Marinated fish roll in flour, fry in butter on both sides until golden brown.

3. Fried fish out onto a plate, sprinkle with finely chopped parsley, and pour the melted butter from the pan. Garnish with lemon slices and serve.

TIP TO THE RECIPE
Garnish can submit potatoes, pickled vegetables , and slices of lemon.

9. Marinated in Lime Juice Grilled Shrimp in Wine Sauce

Serves: 2
Cooking: 30 minutes

ENERGY VALUE PER SERVING
- Calories 717 kcal
- Proteins 32.7 g
- Fats 61.8 g
- Carbohydrates 7.1 g

INGREDIENTS
- 450g Peeled king prawns
- ⅓ cup Lime juice
- 1 tbsp Olive oil
- 120g Butter
- 2 stalks Spring Onion
- 3 cloves Garlic
- 1 cup dry white wine
- pinch Cayenne pepper
- 1 tsp Sea Salt

COOKING INSTRUCTIONS
1. In a bowl, mix shrimp, 1/4 cup of lime juice and olive oil, mix well.
2. In a pan melt the butter, add chopped onion and chopped garlic and saute for 1-2 minutes. Then pour in the wine, add Cayenne pepper, salt, and remaining lime juice. Cook for 3-5 minutes.
3. Heat the grill or barbecue. Fry shrimp about 3 minutes until tender. Place in a bowl with the wine sauce, mix and serve.

10. Octopus garnished with toasted lettuce

Serves: 2
Cooking Time: 25 minutes

ENERGY VALUE PER SERVING
- Calorie 791 kcal
- Proteins of 79.4 g
- Fats 30.7 g
- Carbohydrate 26.6 g

INGREDIENTS
- 2 pieces Squid
- 1 Garlic
- 3 pieces Shallots
- Celery
- Lettuce
- Fresh thyme
- 2 Carrots
- 3 tbsp Olive oil
- 300ml Dry red wine

COOKING INSTRUCTIONS
1. Then, coarsely cut celery, thyme, carrot, shallot, and garlic, but all in a wok, where fry with a little olive oil over medium heat. Thyme can be placed in the whole sprig. It is essentialto fry vegetables properly— this is the secret recipe. Three or four minutes, and you go to the octopus.
2. Pepper, salt — and sand the salt in wardrobe: themselves octopus salt is not necessary. Them and enough salt. It's time to put the wok in the carcass. Fry for 1-2 minutes, pour a glass of dry red wine, cover, and leave for 15-20 minutes. The time depends on the size of the carcass. For medium octopus, 15 minutes is sufficient.
3. Now for the garnish. We break off the top leaves from the lettuce and cut in half the core. In a skillet, warm up olive oil with crushed garlic and place half of the salad down the middle — one or two minutes, no more. It is essential that the leaves retained their crunchy texture and softened.
4. Put on a plate of octopus and fried lettuce, and top with a little olive oil, crushed garlic, and juice, obtained during frying of octopus.
5. Brushing and washing root vegetables, celery, and thyme hold octopus. Remove the beak, eyes, and wash the carcass in cold water. Now, some take them. I do this with the effort of grating the daikon carcass as if unrolling each tentacle — this technology was taught to me by the chef of «Alphabet of taste «William Lamberti. »

11. Sea bass stuffed with vegetables, mussels and saffron oil

Serves: 1
Cooking Time: 40 minutes

ENERGY VALUE PER SERVING
- The caloric value of 729 kcal
- Proteins 82.2 g
- Fats 32.1 g
- Carbohydrates 21.6 g

INGREDIENTS
- 400g Sea bass
- 50g Zucchini
- 60g Fresh asparagus
- 40g Sun-dried tomatoes
- 10ml Olive oil
- 10g Butter
- 5 Mussels
- Small amount Saffron
- Rosemary
- Sea salt to taste
- 50ml White wine
- Ground black pepper to taste
- 100ml Dry white wine
- Salt to taste
- Ground black pepper to taste

COOKING INSTRUCTIONS
1. Seabass Burke, cut off the head and playscheme on the fillet, leaving both fillets and tail. Separately, cut into julienne zucchini, asparagus, sun-dried tomatoes, pickled in olive oil, add the rosemary and put in the sea bass, salt, and pepper. Seabass wrapped in parchment, then wrap in foil and bake 15-20 minutes at 180 degrees.
2. At this time, prepare the sauce: In a saucepan pour the white wine, evaporate for 3-4 minutes, remove from heat and add the butter and saffron. Salt, pepper.
3. Mussels fried in olive oil, salt, and pepper.
4. On a plate lay sea bass next put the molds and pour the sauce around and decorate with rosemary.

12. Mediterranean Mussels with Thyme

Serves: 2
Cooking Time: 20 minutes

ENERGY VALUE PER SERVING
- Calories 372 kcal
- Proteins 48.3 g
- Fats 8 g
- Carbohydrates 13.3 g

INGREDIENTS
- 1 kg Mussels
- 1 clove Shallot Onion
- 4 cloves Garlic
- 1 cup Dry white wine
- Fresh thyme
- Parsley leaves
- Salt to taste

COOKING INSTRUCTIONS
1. If the mussels are frozen, defrost them on the top shelf of the refrigerator.
2. Finely chop the onion and garlic.
3. In a pan throw in the mussels, onion, garlic, whole thyme sprigs, pour the glass of white wine and a glass of water.

4. Put on medium heat cover with a lid and bring to the boil.
5. Once it boils turn off the heat and add the finely Narzan parsley and mix well, the mussels should open up, all unopened mussels discarded. Add salt to taste.
6. With a slotted spoon, put the molds in a deep dish for serving and pour into each plate by ladling the broth, then decorate with sprigs of thyme.

TIP TO THE RECIPE

The secret of good cooking mussels is simple: you can use frozen mussels in shells in their juice. Mussels must be fresh. Molds are not impossible to digest. Just remove the mussels from the heat; you will get the onion and garlic, al dente.

13. Red mullet with Grappa

Serves: 4
Cooking Time: 10 minutes

ENERGY VALUE PER SERVING
- Calories 402 kcal
- Protein 6.1 g
- Fats and 38.1 g
- Carbohydrates 2.8 g

INGREDIENTS
- 4 Red mullets
- 4 tbsp Olive oil
- Fresh thyme
- 1 Shallots
- 80g Butter-
- 1 tsp Mustard
- 3 Tarragon leaves
- 50ml Grappa
- Salt to taste
- Ground black pepper to taste

COOKING INSTRUCTIONS
1. Red mullet, rinse, brush with olive oil, put in each fish at the sprig of thyme, sprinkle with salt and pepper.
2. Place on the grill for five minutes.
3. Ready red mullet on a platter, pour warmed Grappa, and set on fire. Then put on top of butter mixed with mustard and chopped tarragon and onions.

14. Lentils with greens

Serves: 4
Cooking Time: 25 minutes

ENERGY VALUE PER SERVING
- Calories 258 kcal
- Proteins 16.1 g
- Fat 2.1 g
- Carbohydrates 42.1 g

INGREDIENTS
- 150g Puy lentils
- 500g Vegetables
- 2½ Carrots
- 1 Onions
- 1 Leeks
- 1½ pieces Celery
- Fresh thyme
- 3 pieces Shallots
- 1 bunch Spring Onions
- Salt to taste
- Ground black pepper to taste

COOKING INSTRUCTIONS
1. Rinse the lentils in a sieve under cold water, place in a pot, cover with plenty of cold water. Bring to a boil, drain in a colander , and again thoroughly rinsed with cold water.
2. Omit the lentils back into the cleaned pan, add half of the paired vegetables , and 250 ml of cold water.
3. Carrot (2 pieces) peeled and cut in half, onion peel, cut lengthwise and then into quarters, the leek coarsely chop in celery (1 piece) to remove the fiber and cut in half.
4. Add the vegetables and thyme to the lentils. Stir, cover the greaseproof paper, and bring to the boil. Reduce the heat and let lightly boil for 5-8 minutes until the lentil is half cooked. Dry in a sieve to remove the vegetables and thyme.
5. Return the rinsed lentils in a saucepan and add the other half of the paired plants. Add chopped shallots, celery, and carrots, bring to a boil over medium or high heat. Reduce the heat and allow to simmer on low heat without covering with a lid for about 10 minutes, until the liquid will not be exactly two times more than lentils.
6. Add as much oil as you want (for a bit), stir so that the result is a brilliant mixture. Add the herbs, stir, season with salt and pepper. Serve immediately.

15. Salmon skewer with cherry tomatoes in a rosemary marinade

Serves: 4
Cooking Time: 20 minutes

ENERGY VALUE PER SERVING
- Calories 246 kcal
- Protein 26 g
- Fat 12.5 g
- Carbohydrates 5.8g

INGREDIENTS
- 2 tsp Chopped fresh rosemary
- 2 tbsp Olive oil, extra virgin
- 2 cloves Garlic
- 1 tsp Lemon juice
- 1 tsp lemon zest
- 1 tsp Freshly ground black pepper
- 500g Salmon fillet
- 400g Cherry tomatoes

COOKING INSTRUCTIONS
1. Heat the grill or barbecue.
2. In a bowl 6 mix the chopped rosemary, olive oil, chopped garlic, zest and lemon juice, salt, and pepper. Add the chopped small pieces of fish and stir.
3. On skewers, alternating, put cherry tomatoes and pieces of fish.
4. Place on grill and cook, carefully turning, for 4-6 minutes until tender.

16. Stuffed Sardines On Skewers

Serves: 2
Cooking Time: 20 minutes

ENERGY VALUE PER SERVING
- Calorie 530 calories
- Protein 12.5 g
- Fats 30.6 g
- Carbohydrates 53.2 g

INGREDIENTS
- Sardines
- 1 tbsp Pine nuts
- 1 Lemon-
- 1 tbsp Raisins
- 10 pieces Fresh Bay leaf
- 100g Breadcrumbs
- 2 tbsp Olive oil

COOKING INSTRUCTIONS
1. Clean the sardines, remove bones, wash and season with salt.
2. In a pan fry with little olive oil breadcrumbs, raisins, and nuts until golden brown.

3. Roll each carcass of the fish with the mixture. This same mixture to fill the inner part of the sardines and roll it roll. Rolls spread on skewers alternating with Laurel leaves and lemon wedges. Spread on a baking sheet or the surface of the grill, drizzle with olive oil and lemon juice. Bake in preheated to 180-degree oven for 15-20 minutes.
4. A tasty garnish will serve the chickpeas with the tomatoes.

TIP TO THE RECIPE
Instead of pine nuts, you can use almonds or walnuts. And if sardines are delicate, try herring or large pilchards.

17. Skewer of Norwegian Salmon

Serves: 3
Cooking Time: 25 minutes

ENERGY VALUE PER SERVING
- Calories 369 kcal
- Proteins 46.7 g
- Fat 12.1 g
- Carbohydrates 20.9 g

INGREDIENTS
- 600g Norwegian salmon
- 1 Leeks
- 10 pieces Shallots

COOKING INSTRUCTIONS
1. The salmon, onions, and leeks onto the skewers, oiled and fried on the grill.
2. When the fish is cooked through, sprinkle finished skewers with salt and fresh herbs.

18. Lasagna with Turkey Meat and Bechamel Sauce

Serves: 5
Cooking Time: 1 Hour & 15 minutes

ENERGY VALUE PER SERVING
- Calories 780 kcal
- Proteins 56.2 g
- Fats 45.2 g
- Carbohydrates 34.6 g

INGREDIENTS
- 1 kg Minced turkey
- 2 Onion
- 100g Carrots
- 100ml Tomato juice
- 12 Ready-made dry lasagna sheets
- 1L Milk
- 100g Butter
- 100g Wheat flour
- Nutmeg on the tip of a knife
- Ground black pepper to taste
- Salt to taste
- 250g Parmesan cheese

COOKING INSTRUCTIONS

1. In a pan fry the finely chopped onion and beautiful grater carrots, add the beef and mix everything carefully so that the meat wasn't fried a single lump. Then cover with a lid and cook until almost tender. Open the lid— salt and pepper, if desired, you can add Basil or thyme — Turkey is friendly with them and add tomato juice, mix everything thoroughly couple of minutes and remove from the heat and put to cool.
2. Prepare the form in which to bake the lasagna. It is better to take the glass — this is purely from an aesthetic point of view, and basically whatever you have on hand. The bottom and walls of the form grease with butter.
3. Start the Bechamel sauce. In a pan, melt our butter on a small fire that didn't burn. Add flour and mix thoroughly. Add small portions of milk, and mix very thoroughly. Pepper, salt, and of course , added nutmeg — very well, he is suitable for this sauce. The sauce is the consistency should resemble thick cream.

4. Assembly. The bottom of spread a few spoonfuls of sauce and spreadsheets of lasagna, they are part of our stuffing, pour part of the sauce and generously sprinkle with cheese, repeat layers until all the minced meat, the last layer: lasagna sheets, cover with the sauce and top with cheese all fall asleep. A sheet of foil to close the top of the form. Our beauty is ready to go in the oven.
5. 190-200C for half an hour in oven. After half an hour, remove the foil from the brown crust and bake for another 15 minutes.

19. Sautéed Anchovies with Broccoli

Serves: 6
Cooking Time: 25 minutes

THE ENERGY VALUE PER SERVING
- Calories 242 kcal
- Protein 13.8 g
- Fat 9.4 g
- Carbohydrates 32.1 g

INGREDIENTS
- 1.25kg Broccoli
- 30ml Olive oil
- 8 cloves Garlic
- 10 pieces Anchovies
- Salt to taste
- Ground black pepper to taste
- 150g Shell Pasta
- 60g Feta cheese

COOKING INSTRUCTIONS
1. In a hot pan with olive oil, put the chopped into pieces of anchovy filets and chopped garlic. Cook for about 5 minutes until light golden brown.
2. While frying the anchovies, cut off the broccoli stalks. Place the cabbage in a saucepan with plenty of lightly salted boiling water (about 6 liters) and cook for 1 minute.

3. Remove broccoli from water and add to the anchovies into the pan. Cook all together for about 10 minutes until the cabbage is tender, but not lose form.
4. Remove from heat and season with salt and pepper.
5. Boil the horns, as indicated on the package. Horns are ready to drain in a colander. Feta cut into cubes. Mix all the ingredients.

20. Scallops in a Creamy Sauce with Mushrooms and Rice

Serves: 4
Cooking Time: 30 minutes

ENERGY VALUE PER SERVING
- Caloric content of 345 kcal
- Proteins 23.7 g
- Fat 24.1 g
- Carbohydrates 11.1 g

INGREDIENTS
- 3 tbsp Butter
- 450g Scallops
- 340g Fresh mushrooms
- 50g Spring onion
- Cayenne pepper pinch
- 1 tbsp Wheat flour
- 230g Shelly juice
- 100ml Whipped cream
- Rice to taste

COOKING INSTRUCTIONS
1. Melt the butter in a large frying pan over high heat. Scallops salt and pepper and place on pan. Cook for about 5 minutes. Place it into a bowl.

2. Reduce heat to medium. Add the chopped mushrooms, 0.5 Cup of chopped green onions , and Cayenne pepper. Cook for about 6 minutes until golden brown. Sprinkle with flour and cook for another 30 seconds. Shelly then stir in juice and cream. Simmer until the sauce thickens, occasionally stirring, 10 minutes. Add the scallops and cook for 1 minute. Season with salt and pepper.
3. Cook rice and spread out on plates or bowls. Then put the scallops, and sprinkle the remaining green onions.

21. Pork Stew with Celery, Carrots, Madeira Wine and Spices

Serves: 4
Cooking: 1 hour & 15 minutes

ENERGY VALUE PER SERVING
- Calories 386 kcal
- Proteins 33.6 g
- Fat 17 g
- Carbohydrates 19.5 g

INGREDIENTS
- 6 pieces Celery
- 900g Pork fillet
- 2 Onions
- 3 cloves Garlic
- 400g Canned tomatoes
- Ground black pepper to taste
- Thyme spice
- Salt to taste
- 1 tsp Ground coryza
- 1 tsp Ground coriander
- 200g Canned green peas
- 300g Carrots
- 1 tsp Rosmarin
- 125g Madera
- 2 Bay leaf
- 2 tbsp Vegetable oil

COOKING INSTRUCTIONS
1. Cut the pork meat into cubes (2.5-3 cm) and sprinkle with salt and pepper.
2. Peel the carrots, one half of which is cut in large slices, and the second finely chop. Finely chop the onion and garlic. Celery stalks cut into slices.
3. Preheat a large deep pan and in hot oil fry the pork, stirring constantly. After about 10-12 minutes, remove the meat and place in a bowl.
4. In the same pan saute for about 5-7 minutes and finely chopped vegetables, pre-draining from the pan nearly all the grease. Add the spices, juniper berries, and continue to sauté for 1 more minute.
5. Pour in sautéed vegetables Madeira and bring to a boil, continuing to stir.
6. Return the meat to the pan; add canned tomatoes, and large slices of carrots. Again, bring everything to a boil and cook over moderate heat, stirring occasionally.
7. After about half an hour, when the liquid will thicken, and the meat will become soft, throw in the stew peas, stir and simmer for another 5 minutes.
8. Before serving, remove the Bay leaves from the stew and let stand at least 15 minutes. As a side dish — boiled potatoes.

22. Fillet of Seabass with Asparagus Wrapped in Bacon

Serves: 1
Cooking Time: 30 minutes

ENERGY VALUE PER SERVING
- Calories 524 kcal
- Proteins of 55.5 g
- Fats 30.2 g
- Carbohydrates 8.6 g

INGREDIENTS
- 1 Fillet seabass on the skin
- 50g Fresh asparagus
- 50g Bacon
- Fresh thyme
- 1 Corn tortillas
- 1 Tomatoes-
- 30g Peeled shrimp
- 10g Pickled capers

COOKING INSTRUCTIONS
1. Sea bass fillets dry sprinkle with lemon juice, olive oil sprinkled with chopped garlic, set aside in a cold place for 10-15 minutes.

2. In hot oil, put five cloves of garlic and a sprig of thyme, fry, and drain. To the resulting oil to fry the fillets not more than 1 minute on each side. Discard in Safeco. Put in a preheated 140C oven for 5-7 minutes.
3. Asparagus wash, dry.
4. Bacon fry in butter for 1-2 minutes, gently aside. Oil from under the bacon stir-fry the asparagus, wrap it in bacon.
5. Serve with capers, Mexican cake, pre-dried, pan-fried, and tartare of shrimp in stewed tomatoes.

23. Spaghetti Squash with Sun-Dried Tomatoes

Serves: 5
Cooking Time: 1 Hour & 15 minutes

ENERGY VALUE PER SERVING
- Calories 372 kcal
- Proteins 11.5 g
- Fats 19.8 g
- Carbohydrates 52.5 g

INGREDIENTS
- 1 Pumpkin squash
- 4 stalks of Oregano
- 2 cloves of Garlic
- 5 pieces of Sun-dried tomatoes
- 3 Green basil
- 25g of Parmesan cheese
- 80ml of Olive oil
- Salt to taste
- Freshly ground black pepper

COOKING INSTRUCTIONS
1. Like any vegetable, spaghetti squash can be cooked whole, and then to keep it in the oven will have twice as long. It will be faster if you cut it in half. Only need a sharp and long knife — the raw flesh of the squash is very elastic. Scrape the white pith and the seeds and put aside.

2. The halves of the squash should be watered and sprinkle all aromatic: it can be any set of herbs and spices like olive oil, salt and freshly ground black pepper, grated garlic and the leaves from a couple of sprigs of fresh oregano. At the end of all of this to massage into the flesh
3. Lay the pumpkin halves on a foil-covered cookie sheet flesh down. Put in a preheated 175-degree oven. In about an hour (more or less depending on the weight of the vegetable) it will reach the desired condition — plug should be easy to get in the flesh.
4. While baking the squash, scrubbing apart the core of the pumpkin and remove the seeds. Throw them in a well-heated pan, sprinkle a pinch of salt and, continually stirring, fry the seeds until Golden brown .
5. After an hour, remove the squash from the oven, let it cool slightly , and flip the flesh upside. Now each half is necessary to scrape with a fork — you will see how it will come out quite long noodles, the spaghetti, the origin of the vegetable.
6. In a large saucepan heat with a little oil, put it in the inside of the squash and add halved sun-dried tomatoes. The tomatoes have to choose softer and juicier, and it is better to do it yourself: cut in half, lay on a baking sheet flesh up, season with salt and pepper, drizzle with olive oil, and leave overnight in a preheated 80-degree oven.

7. When squash and tomatoes are warmed, add the fresh Basil leaves (large leaves can tear with your hands) and a handful of grated Parmesan or Pecorino. Mix the vegetables with cheese and hold for a few seconds on the fire.
8. Spread the cooked vegetables on plates, pour fresh olive oil, add more cheese, salt, freshly ground black pepper, a few basil leaves, some crispy roasted sunflower seeds — all optional and in any proportions. And serve.

Chapter 8 - Mediterranean Recipes for Sauces and Marinades

1. Lemon marinade with thyme and shallots for fish

Serves: 4
Cooking Time: 45 minutes

ENERGY VALUE PER SERVING
- Calorie 119 kcal
- Protein 1.5 g
- Fats 9.9 g
- Carbohydrates 5.2 g

INGREDIENTS
- 3 tbsp Dry white wine
- 3 tbsp Lemon juice
- 2 tbsp Olive oil, extra virgin
- Fresh thyme
- 2 pieces Shallots
- 1 Lemon
- Coarse salt to taste
- Freshly ground black pepper to taste

COOKING INSTRUCTIONS

1. In a bowl , mix lemon juice, white wine , and olive oil. Pour into the form.
2. In the marinade, put the fish pieces, stir in the thyme sprigs and sliced lemon circles, sprinkle with finely chopped shallots. Cover with plastic wrap and send it at some time in the refrigerator, turning occasionally.
3. Salt and pepper the fish and grill or barbecue until cooked.

2. Barbecue sauce for shrimp on the grill

Serves: 4
Cooking Time: 30 minutes

ENERGY VALUE PER SERVING
- Calories 137.5 kcal
- Protein 1.8 g
- Fat 4.6 g
- Carbohydrates 24.2 g

INGREDIENTS
- 2 tsp of Canola oil
- 240g of Onions
- 2 cloves of Garlic
- ¾ cups of Water
- ½ cups of Chili sauce
- 2 tbsp of Red wine vinegar
- 2tsp of Ground chili
- 340ml of Coca-Cola
- 1 Jalapeno pepper

COOKING INSTRUCTIONS
1. Heat the oil in a small saucepan over medium heat. Add chopped onion and chopped garlic. Cook, stirring, for 2 minutes, until the onions become soft. Add water, chili sauce, vinegar, chili powder, Coca-Cola , and chopped jalapenos. Bring to a boil, reduce heat, and simmer about 12 minutes until the volume is reduced to 1.5 cups.
2. Pour half the sauce into the blender and chop. Pour into a jar. Repeat the same with remaining sauce. Store in the refrigerator.

TIP TO THE RECIPE

This sauce is more suitable for dipping, not for lubrication before frying. Try this sauce with grilled shrimp.

3. Marinade with olive oil and herbs

Serves: 4
Cooking Time: 1 hour

ENERGY VALUE PER SERVING
- Calories 138 kcal
- Protein 0.6 g
- Fat 14 g
- Carbohydrates 2.9 gr

INGREDIENTS
- ⅓ cup Extra virgin olive oil
- Fresh rosemary
- Fresh thyme
- 3 cloves Garlic
- 2 tbsp Red wine vinegar
- Freshly ground black pepper to taste

COOKING INSTRUCTIONS
1. In a bowl , mix olive oil, chopped rosemary, chopped thyme, chopped garlic, vinegar, and a little black pepper.
2. Add the meat and send it to marinate in the fridge for 3 hours–overnight.

TIP TO THE RECIPE
A great marinade for any meat and poultry.

4. The Marinade Made of White Wine with Oregano and Garlic

Serves: 4
Cooking Time: 28 minutes

ENERGY VALUE PER PORTION
- Caloricity 110 kcal
- Protein 0.8 g
- Fats 9.3 g
- Carbohydrate 2.8 g

INGREDIENTS
- ⅓ cups White dry wine
- ½ cups Lemon juice
- 2 tbsp Extra virgin
- 2 cloves Garlic
- 1 tbsp Dried oregano
- 1 tsp Salt
- ½ tsp Freshly ground black pepper

COOKING INSTRUCTIONS
1. In a bowl, mix lemon juice, white wine, olive oil, chopped garlic, and oregano. Salt and pepper.

TIP TO THE RECIPE
This is an excellent marinade for fish, chicken, shrimp, and vegetables. Leave a small amount of the marinade and put the meat and vegetables during grilling.

5. Garlic seasoning for grilled meat

Serves: 4
Cooking: 52 minutes

ENERGY VALUE PER SERVING
- Calories 5 kcal
- Protein 1.5 g
- Fat 5.1 g
- Carbohydrates 6.7 g

INGREDIENTS
- 8 cloves of Garlic
- 1 tbsp of Olive oil extra virgin
- 2 tsp of Mustard
- 1½ tsp of Large salt
- Freshly ground black
- Grated lemon

COOKING INSTRUCTIONS
1. In a small bowl, combine chopped garlic, olive oil, mustard, salt, pepper ,and lemon zest. With your hands spread the meat and leave for 2 hours– overnight, then fry on the grill.

TIP TO THE RECIPE
This seasoning is great for chicken, pork, lamb, beef, and seafood.

6. Yogurt marinade with herbs and spices for Moroccan

Serves: 4
Cooking Time: 55 minutes

ENERGY VALUE PER SERVING
- Calories 68 kcal
- Protein 1.8 g
- Fat 5.1 g
- Carbohydrates 5 gr

INGREDIENTS
- ¼ cup Chopped parsley
- ¼ cup Natural nonfat yogurt
- 2 tbsp Chopped cilantro (coriander)
- 1 tbsp Extra virgin olive oil1
- 2 tbsp Lemon juice
- 3 cloves Garlic
- 1½ tsp Paprika
- 1 tsp Ground cumin
- ¼ tsp Salt
- Freshly ground black pepper

COOKING INSTRUCTIONS
1. In a bowl , mix yogurt, parsley, cilantro, lemon juice, olive oil, chopped garlic, paprika, and cumin. Season with salt and pepper.

TIP TO THE RECIPE
This is an excellent marinade for chicken and grilled tuna. The amount of marinade is designed for 500 grams of chicken or fish fillet.

7. Parsley oil

Serves: 4
Cooking Time: 30 minutes

ENERGY VALUE PER PORTION
- Caloricity 112 kcal
- Protein 0.9 g
- Fats 11.6 g
- Carbohydrates 1.9 g

INGREDIENTS
- Coarse salt to taste
- 2 bunches Parsley
- ¼ cup Extra Virgin Olive Oil

COOKING INSTRUCTIONS
1. Tear off the leaves of parsley.
2. Bring the salt water to a boil in a saucepan. Add parsley leaves, leaving 2 tablespoons. Cook for about 20 seconds, then quickly transfer to ice water.
3. Drain and transfer to a blender. Grind until mashed.
4. Put the mashed potatoes in cheesecloth, folded in several layers, and squeeze the juice.
5. In a bowl, mix parsley juice, olive oil, and a little salt.
6. Pour into a bottle and add the left fresh parsley leaves. Keep in the refrigerator.

Chapter 9 Snacks Mediterranean Cuisine

1. Spicy tomato dip to baked potatoes

Serves: 4
Cooking Time: 30 minutes

ENERGY VALUE PER PORTION
- Caloricity 59 kcal
- Protein 2 g
- Fat 2.5 g
- Carbohydrates 7.6 g

INGREDIENTS
- ½ tbsp Extra virgin olive oil
- 6 cloves Garlic
- 420g Canned tomatoes sliced
- ½ tsp Smoked paprika
- ½ tsp Red pepper flakes
- ¼ tsp Salt

COOKING INSTRUCTIONS
1. Heat olive oil in a saucepan. Add chopped garlic and sauté for 1 minute.
2. Then add the tomatoes, paprika, red pepper flakes, and salt. Stir and cook for about 15–20 minutes, until the sauce is thickened to a ketchup state

TIP TO THE RECIPE
Serve with charcoal-baked or oven-baked potatoes.

2. Green beans with warm dressing and bacon

Serves: 2
Cooking Time: 30 minutes

ENERGY VALUE PER PORTION
- Caloricity 140 kcal
- Protein 7.3 g
- Fats 9.2 g
- Carbohydrate 7.3 g

INGREDIENTS
- 2 pieces Bacon
- 1 Shallot
- 230g Green String Beans
- 2 tsp White wine vinegar

COOKING INSTRUCTIONS
1. Cook the beans, chopped into small pieces, in boiling salted water until soft, about 8 minutes. Drain and transfer to a bowl.
2. Meanwhile, sauté the chopped bacon in a well-heated skillet over medium heat until crisp. Put on a paper towel.
3. Put the finely chopped shallots into the pan and sauté for 30 seconds. Remove from heat and cool slightly. Add vinegar, salt, and pepper.
4. Pour beans with warm dressing and lay on top slices of bacon.

3. Rolls with lettuce

Serves: 2
Cooking Time: 20 minutes

ENERGY VALUE PER PORTION
- Caloricity 267 kcal
- Proteins 25.2 g
- Fats 17.2 g
- Carbohydrates 1.4 g

INGREDIENTS
- Green salad to taste
- 2 Egg
- 200g Hard cheese
- 200g Peeled shrimp
- Low-calorie Mayonnaise to taste

COOKING INSTRUCTIONS
1. Prepare the filling for rolls. Boil eggs and finely crush or grate. Grate the cheese. Finely chop the shrimp. Add some mayonnaise.
2. Put the cooked mass on lettuce leaves.
3. Gently wrap lettuce in rolls.

4. Baked tomatoes with Provencal herbs

Serves: 2
Cooking Time: 25 minutes

ENERGY VALUE PER SERVING
- Calories 221 kcal
- Protein 1.5 g
- Fat 20.5 g
- Carbohydrates 8.9 g

INGREDIENTS
- 4 Tomatoes
- 2 tbsp Olive oil
- Salt to taste
- Ground black pepper to taste
- 1 tsp Mixed Herbs

COOKING INSTRUCTIONS
1. Put the tomatoes in the oven for 15-20 minutes at 180 degrees. Plants are ideal when a little cracked, but not turn into puree. In the end, you can turn on the oven for 3 minutes.
2. Drizzle the tomatoes with oil, sprinkle with salt, pepper, and herbs.

5. Hummus with roasted peppers

Serves: 4
Cooking Time: 15 minutes

ENERGY VALUE PER SERVING
- Calories 221 kcal
- Whites 6.2 g
- The fats of 16.2 g
- Carbohydrates 12.3 g

INGREDIENTS
- 1 Canned jar chickpeas
- 1 Fresh red bell peppers
- 2 tbsp Tahini
- Lemon pieces
- 30ml Olive oil

COOKING INSTRUCTIONS
1. Preheat the oven to 200 degrees.
2. Bake the red pepper for about 20 minutes, then flip and bake for another 20 minutes.
3. Remove from the oven and place it in a plastic container with a sealed lid immediately and store it in the refrigerator for 2 hours.
4. Drain the liquid from the chickpeas.
5. Remove the skin from the pepper and coarsely chop.
6. Mix in a food processor the chickpeas, red pepper, tahini , and lemon juice.

7. Gradually add olive oil to achieve the desired degree of density.
8. Serve with pitas or pita bread.

TIP TO THE RECIPE
This hummus turns softer taste and less like traditional hummus. It also requires less olive oil because of the liquid which is contained in pepper.

6. Octopus Carpaccio

Serves: 1
Cooking Time: 15 minutes

ENERGY VALUE PER SERVING
- Calories 279 kcal
- Proteins 18.4 g
- Fats 16 g
- Carbohydrates 14.7 g

INGREDIENTS
- 80g Tentacle of the octopus
- 15g Rocket
- 15g Sun-dried tomatoes in oil
- 10g Black olives
- 20g Avocado
- 2g Green onion
- 10ml Olive oil
- 2ml Balsamic vinegar
- 2ml Lemon juice
- 0.2g Pink pepper
- 10g Ciabatta
- 2g Garlic

COOKING INSTRUCTIONS
1. Boil the octopus (to lower the tentacles into the boiling water at the end to salt).
2. Boiled octopus slice and put it on the plate.
3. Season with olive oil, lemon juice, and balsamic vinegar.
4. Put the arugula, dressed with olive oil, salt, pepper.
5. Diced avocado, green onions, and black olives ring.
6. Place them on a dish, add the sun-dried tomatoes, sprinkle top with crushed crackers ciabatta.
7. Decorate with lettuce leaves.

7. The Babaganoush with Roasted Peppers

Serves: 2
Cooking Time: 30 minutes

ENERGY VALUE PER SERVING
- Calories 176 kcal
- Protein 6.5 g
- Fats 11.2 g
- Carbohydrates 12.1 g

INGREDIENTS
- 2 Eggplants
- 2 Fresh red chilli
- 3 tbsp Tahini
- 1 Lemon-
- 1 tbsp Paprika

COOKING INSTRUCTIONS
1. Preheat the oven to 180 degrees.
2. Eggplant fry in a hot pan grill to black markings and bake in the oven for 40 minutes, pre-pinhole with a fork.
3. After 20 minutes, add red pepper. Remove from the oven and place in a plastic container and store in the refrigerator.
4. The flesh of the eggplant, remove with a spoon from the peel and finely chop.

5. Pepper peel and white films and also cut into small pieces and mix with eggplant. Add fresh tachini and lemon juice to pasta (do not be afraid that it will be too sour, as the eggplant will absorb it) and mix well. Sprinkle with paprika powder.
6. Serve as a snack, on a side dish to grilled meat or with pitas.

TIP TO THE RECIPE

For babaganoush vegetables, it is better to bake in advance the night before. You can also add chopped cilantro, green onions, or mint.

8. Olives with Orange Zest, Cumin, and Caraway Seeds

Serves: 4
Cooking Time: 30 minutes

ENERGY VALUE PER SERVING
- Calories 181 kcal
- Proteins 1.5g
- Fat 17.1 g
- Carbohydrates 8.4 g

INGREDIENTS
- 2 tsp Cumin seeds
- 1 tsp Cumin seeds
- Red pepper
- 3 Oranges, zested
- 2 tbsp Extra virgin Olive oil
- 2 cups Olive oil

COOKING INSTRUCTIONS
1. In a small bowl, lightly grind cumin seeds, then add cumin, red pepper flakes, and olive oil.
2. Add the olives and mix well. Leave it for a while.

9. Cheese Baskets with Mussels

Serves: 8
Cooking Time: 40 minutes

ENERGY VALUE PER SERVING
- Calories 111 kcal
- Proteins 9.1 g
- Fat 7.5 g
- Carbohydrates 0.6 g

INGREDIENTS
- 350g Frozen mussels
- 100g Grated Parmesan cheese
- 2 Baku cucumbers
- 1 tbsp Vegetable oil
- 8 Quail egg
- 20g Arugula
- 1tbsp Lemon juice

COOKING INSTRUCTIONS
1. Prepare the pastry: the Cup bottom diameter 5-6 cm, cut the A4 sheet of paper a circle with diameter 2 times more glass, grate cheese on a fine grater. Over medium heat preheat the pan, remove from heat, add cheese, allow to melt and cool slightly, then place on the bottom of the glass to form the shape. Baskets ready!

2. Prepare the mussels: wipe the pan, add 1 tbsp oil, to evaporate the liquid from the molds, pour lemon juice. The mussels are ready, allow them to cool.
3. Eggs boiled and cut into 2-4 pieces. Cucumbers cut into strips.
4. To complete cooking before serving. Toppings: onion, cucumber, mayonnaise, mix, and put in baskets. Decorate eggs and greens!

10. Scallops under the Pear Pesto

Serves: 2
Cooking Time: 30 minutes

ENERGY VALUE PER SERVING
- Caloric value of 165 kcal
- Protein 10.5 g
- Fats 8.5 g
- Carbohydrates-12.7 g

INGREDIENTS
- 3 Scallops
- 1 Pear
- 3 Cherry tomatoes
- Basil leaves
- 1 tbsp Pine nuts
- 10 ml Olive oil
- 1 clove garlic, finely chopped
- Salt to taste

COOKING INSTRUCTIONS
1. Pear wash, dry, cut small cubes.
2. The pan heat, pour a little olive oil, put the bag. Add a little water and simmer for 10-15 minutes.
3. The scallops are rinsed, dried with a paper towel, season with salt, put in a pan with the peas, sauté 4-6 minutes.

4. Basil washed, dried, placed in a container, add the pine nuts, chopped garlic, olive oil, and carefully beat with a blender until a homogeneous mass.
5. Prepared scallops on a platter, garnish of stewed pears obtained with pesto, thinly sliced tomatoes ,and sprig of Basil. 6. Serve, enjoy a meal ,and dream about the sea.

11. Zucchini in Greek

Serves: 2
Cooking Time: 40 minutes

ENERGY VALUE PER SERVING
- Calorific value 136 kcal
- Protein 1.5 g
- Fat 10.3 g
- Carbohydrates 10 g

INGREDIENTS
- 120g Zucchini
- 5g Wheat flour
- 1 Onion
- 20g Spinach
- 20ml Vegetable oil
- 10g Green salad
- 20g Sweet pepper
- Parsley
- 1 Tomatoes
- Pinch of Salt,
- Pinch of Sugar

COOKING INSTRUCTIONS
1. Clean young squash peeled, cut into neat slices thickness of about 1 cm. Put on the table a little flour and roll it, slice zucchini. Saute on a low heat until golden brown.

2. Chop the green onion, fry it in vegetable oil. Then add the onions chopped spinach, lettuce, bell pepper, parsley, tomatoes , and cook vegetable mixture for 10-15 minutes.
3. Season the boiled vegetables with salt and pepper, and then pour this mixture into the courgettes and cook all together in the oven for 15-20 minutes.
4. Cool the squash and serve sprinkled with chopped dill.

Chapter 10 Drinks Mediterranean Cuisine

1. Smoothie pineapple raspberry

Serves: 4
Cooking Time: 20 minutes

ENERGY VALUE PER SERVING
- Calories 178 kcal
- Protein 2.9 g
- Fat - 1.4 g
- Carbohydrates 37.3 g

INGREDIENTS
- 700g Pineapple
- 300g Frozen raspberries
- 300ml Vanilla rice milk
- 3 tbsp Buckwheat flakes
- Mint to taste

COOKING INSTRUCTIONS
1. Pineapple chunk peels and removes the core. Cut into medium pieces.
2. Put the raspberries can be frozen can be defrosted during the night on the top shelf of the refrigerator.

3. Take 200 ml of rice milk (in the absence of it, of course, you can substitute no fat milk), buckwheat flakes, slices of Mandarin , and pineapple and punch at high speed in a blender.
4. Let stand for about 10-15 minutes — during this time, the oat flakes will swell.
5. Add another 100 ml of rice drink and a punch in the blender again. If the smoothie is still thick, bring the water or rice drink to need concentration.
6. Garnish with leaves of fresh mint.

TIP TO THE RECIPE

Buckwheat flakes can be replaced by oat or any other, to taste.

2. Beet-pineapple smoothie with fennel

Serves: 2
Cooking Time: 10 minutes

ENERGY VALUE PER SERVING
- Calorific value 136 kcal
- Protein 3.1 g
- Fats 0.5 g
- Carbohydrates 29.5 g

INGREDIENTS
- 300g Beets
- 1/3 Pineapple
- 1 Fennel
- 1 Lime

COOKING INSTRUCTIONS
1. Clean ⅓ of the pineapple and remove the core.
2. Clean the beets and squeeze the juice of fennel. 3. Squeeze the juice of a lime.
3. Put all the ingredients in a blender and run at maximum speed until smooth.

3. Grape smoothie with green tea

Serves: 2
Cooking Time: 25 minutes

ENERGY VALUE PER SERVING
- Calories 109 kcal
- Protein 1 g
- Fat 0.4 g
- Carbohydrates 27.2 g

INGREDIENTS
- 125ml Water
- 250g Green seedless grapes
- 125g Pineapple
- 6 Ice cubes
- 1 tsp Green tea

COOKING INSTRUCTIONS
1. Pour green tea with hot (but not boiling) water. Cover and let it brew for 5 minutes. Strain and cool completely.
2. Place all the ingredients in the blender bowl: grapes, pineapple slices, tea, and ice cubes. Beat until smooth.
3. Pour into a glass and serve immediately.

4. Black cream smoothie

Serves: 1
Cooking: 5 minutes

ENERGY VALUE PER PORTION
- Caloricity 208 kcal
- Proteins 3.9 g
- Fats 0.9 g
- Carbohydrates 49.2 g

INGREDIENTS
- Frozen blueberries to taste
- 1 Bananas
- 2 Strawberry
- 2.5ml Cream
- 5g Oatmeal

COOKING INSTRUCTIONS
1. Place fruits and cereals in a blender.
2. Beat.
3. Put in a glass.
4. Add cream.

5. Berry cranberry and blackberry smoothie

Serves: 2
Cooking Time: 5 minutes

ENERGY VALUE PER PORTION
- Caloricity 201 kcal
- Protein 7.3 g
- Fats 3.5 g
- Carbohydrates 36.8 g

INGREDIENTS
- ½ cup Cranberry fruit drink
- 160g Cranberries
- 190g Blackberry
- 250g Raspberry yogurt

COOKING INSTRUCTIONS
1. Beat in a blender until smooth all the ingredients, adding a little ice.
2. Pour into glasses and serve.

6. Blueberry Shake with Honey

Serves: 4
Cooking Time: 25 minutes

ENERGY VALUE PER PORTION
- Caloricity 72 kcal
- Protein 2.8 g
- Fat 2.2 g
- Carbohydrates 9.6 g

INGREDIENTS
- 2 tbsp Honey 2 tablespoons
- 100g Blueberries 100 g
- 125ml Milk 125 ml
- 125g Natural yogurt 125 g
- 5 Ice cubes 5 pieces

COOKING INSTRUCTIONS
1. All ingredients are put in a blender bowl (do not defrost frozen berries beforehand) and grind.

7. Raspberry cooler with lemon

Serves: 4
Cooking Time: 30 minutes

ENERGY VALUE PER PORTION
- Caloricity 139 kcal
- Protein 1.7 g
- Fats 0.8 g
- Carbohydrates 28.4 g

INGREDIENTS
- 1 Lemon
- 720g Raspberry
- 1 Vanilla pod
- ¼ cups Sugar
- 3 cups Sparkling water

COOKING INSTRUCTIONS
1. In a bowl, mix the berries, sliced into thin slices of lemon, vanilla pod, from which remove the seeds and put the same in the beans and sugar. Put in a water bath and cook, stirring, for about 12 minutes, until the berries give away the juice.
2. Wipe the mass through a sieve, squeezing all the juice. Chill.
3. Pour the syrup into 3 ice-filled glasses and fill it with sparkling water. Serve immediately, garnishing with lemon slices.

Conclusion

The best recipes for low-calorie Mediterranean diet food have been compiled for you. Calories calculated for raw foods. 101 Mediterranean recipes! Our work is aimed at facilitating the lives of people. We give answers to questions - ready-made solutions!

Adhere to this style of nutrition, and your life will change. You will feel better; your mood and tone will rise. This is the first part of the book. We will work to improve our books, for the benefit of you!

Made in the USA
Monee, IL
02 January 2020